SNOW-FRINGED FIRS ON VANCOUVER ISLAND.

A MEADOW AT 5,000 FEET ON THE HURRICANE RIDGE TRAIL

THE SOUTH WALL OF MOUNT DECEPTION

SAND DUNES ENGULFING THE PINES ALONG THE OREGON SHORE

BULL ELK JOUSTING IN THE HOH VALLEY RAIN FOREST

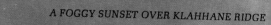

NIGHTFALL ON SANDSTONE STACKS ON THE WASHINGTON COAST

TIME
LIFE
BOOKS

AMERICA'S NORTHWEST COAST

THE WORLD'S WILD PLACES/TIME-LIFE BOOKS/AMSTERDAM

BY RICHARD L. WILLIAMS
AND THE EDITORS OF TIME-LIFE BOOKS

THE WORLD'S WILD PLACES

EDITOR: Charles Osborne
Editorial Staff for *America's Northwest Coast*:
Editor: Harvey B. Loomis
Picture Editor: Jane Scholl
Designer: Charles Mikolaycak
Staff Writers: Sam Halper,
Timberlake Wertenbaker
Chief Researcher: Martha T. Goolrick
Researchers: Joan Chambers, Muriel Clarke,
Carol Clingan, John Hamlin,
Villette Harris, Beatrice Hsia
Design Assistant: Vincent Lewis

ISBN 7054 0381 5

Published by Time-Life Books (Nederland) B.V.
Ottho Heldringstraat 5, Amsterdam 1018.

The Author: For Richard Lippincott Williams, writing *America's Northwest Coast* has meant the native's return. Though in recent years an Easterner, he was born in Seattle and until he was 30 thought of the Midwest as "back East." He has been a writer, editor and correspondent with the *Seattle Times*, Dell Publishing Co., and TIME and LIFE magazines. For TIME-LIFE BOOKS he was the editor of the LIFE Library of Photography as well as the 27-volume Foods of the World series.

The Cover: Two sea stacks, part of a cluster of 50- to 100-foot-high rocks called Giants' Graveyard, are silhouetted against the sunset over Teahwhit Head (*far right*) on the Olympic Peninsula in Washington. A familiar sight along the Northwest coast, these stacks are all that remain of rocky headlands that have been eroded away by the Pacific. The stacks, too, will eventually succumb to the pounding sea.

Contents

Where Mountains Meet the Sea

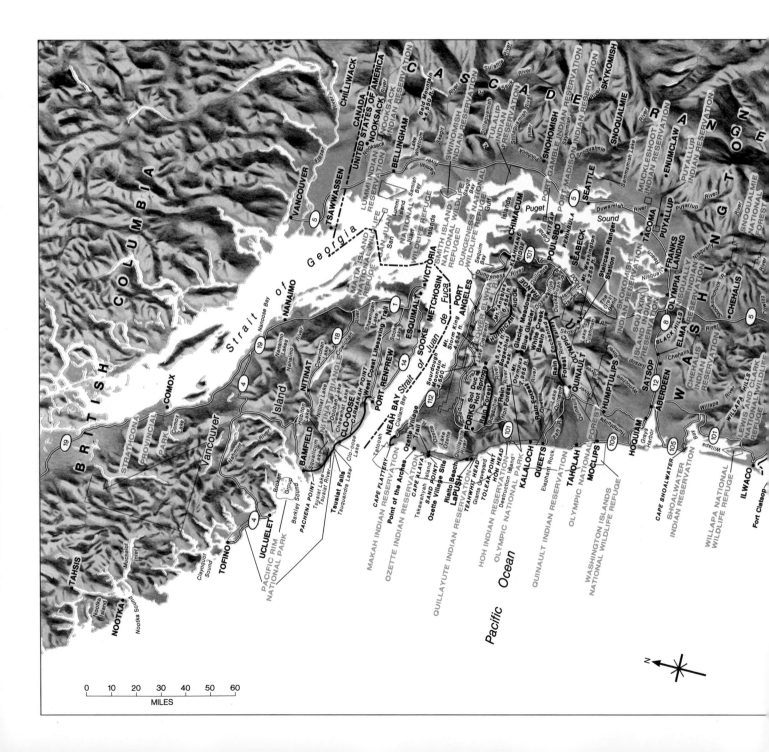

CANADA
UNITED STATES OF AMERICA

CASCADE RANGE

BRITISH COLUMBIA

Strait of Georgia

Vancouver Island

WASHINGTON

Puget Sound

Strait of Juan de Fuca

Pacific Ocean

CHILLIWACK
NOOKSACK INDIAN RESERVATION
BELLINGHAM
LUMMI INDIAN RESERVATION
Lummi Island
San Juan Island
SAN JUAN ISLANDS NATIONAL WILDLIFE REFUGE
MATIA ISLAND NATIONAL WILDLIFE REFUGE
SMITH ISLAND NATIONAL WILDLIFE REFUGE
DUNGENESS NATIONAL WILDLIFE REFUGE
VICTORIA
ESQUIMALT
METCHOSIN
PORT ANGELES
CHIMACUM
PORT GAMBLE
PORT MADISON INDIAN RESERVATION
POULSBO
SEABECK
KITSAP
SEATTLE
TACOMA
PUYALLUP
SWINOMISH INDIAN RESERVATION
SNOHOMISH
TULALIP INDIAN RESERVATION
STILLAGUAMISH INDIAN RESERVATION
MUCKLESHOOT INDIAN RESERVATION
PUYALLUP INDIAN RESERVATION
SNOQUALMIE
ENUMCLAW
FRANKS LANDING
SQUAXIN ISLAND INDIAN RESERVATION
SKYKOMISH
SNOQUALMIE NATIONAL FOREST

VANCOUVER
TSAWWASSEN
NANAIMO
COMOX
STRATHCONA PROVINCIAL PARK
NITINAT
CLO-OOSE
BAMFIELD
PACHENA POINT
Tsusiat Falls
UCLUELET
TOFINO
PACIFIC RIM NATIONAL PARK
NOOTKA
TAHSIS
Nootka Island
Nootka Sound
Clayoquot Sound
Barkley Sound
Broken Group

PORT RENFREW
SOOKE
NEAH BAY
CAPE FLATTERY
Point of the Arches
MAKAH INDIAN RESERVATION
Tatoosh
Ozette Village
CAPE ALAVA
SAND POINT
OZETTE INDIAN RESERVATION
Ozette Village Site
Takawahyah Island
Ozette Lake
Rialto Beach
LaPUSH
TEAHWHIT HEAD
QUILLAYUTE INDIAN RESERVATION
Giants Graveyard
TOLEAK POINT
HOH HEAD
Destruction Island
HOH INDIAN RESERVATION
OLYMPIC NATIONAL PARK
FORKS
Sol Duc Hot Springs
Rain Forest
Bogachiel River
Hoh River
KALALOCH
Elephant Rock
QUEETS
TAHOLAH
MOCLIPS
QUINAULT INDIAN RESERVATION
QUINAULT
HUMPTULIPS
SATSOP
ABERDEEN
HOQUIAM
Grays Harbor
OLYMPIC NATIONAL FOREST
WASHINGTON ISLANDS NATIONAL WILDLIFE REFUGE
Mt. Olympus 7,965 ft.
Mt. Anderson 6,540 ft.
Mt. Washington 6,255 ft.
Staircase Ranger Station
Rain Forest
Olympic
LOWER ELWHA
HURRICANE RIDGE
Glacier Meadows
Blue Glacier
Enchanted Valley
SKOKOMISH INDIAN RESERVATION
BLACK HILLS
OLYMPIA
ELMA
SQUAXIN ISLAND INDIAN RESERVATION
CHEHALIS INDIAN RESERVATION
CHEHALIS
WILLAPA HILLS
LEWIS AND CLARK NATIONAL WILDLIFE REFUGE
CAPE SHOALWATER
SHOALWATER INDIAN RESERVATION
WILLAPA NATIONAL WILDLIFE REFUGE
Willapa Bay
ILWACO
Fort Clatsop

Storm King Mtn. 4,534 ft.
Sourdough Mtn. 3,560 ft.
Bald Mountain 4,550 ft.

0 10 20 30 40 50 60
MILES

N

The Northwest coast as described in this book extends some 600 miles in a narrow strip from Vancouver Island in British Columbia south to the Oregon-California border. Buttressed by mountains of the Coast Ranges and battered by the Pacific's relentless surge, the area has a stunning variety of natural features, from the glacier-clad Olympic peaks to shadowy rain forests to scalloped tidal pools at the sea's edge. Civilization intrudes on much of the region, but in places like the Siskiyou National Forest in Oregon, Washington's Olympic Peninsula and the rugged coast of Vancouver Island the wildness endures. The many rivers are shown in blue on the map below; trails mentioned by the author are in black. Red lines enclose national parks and forests, Indian reservations and wildlife refuges. Black squares denote places of special interest and blue dots trace scenic waterways.

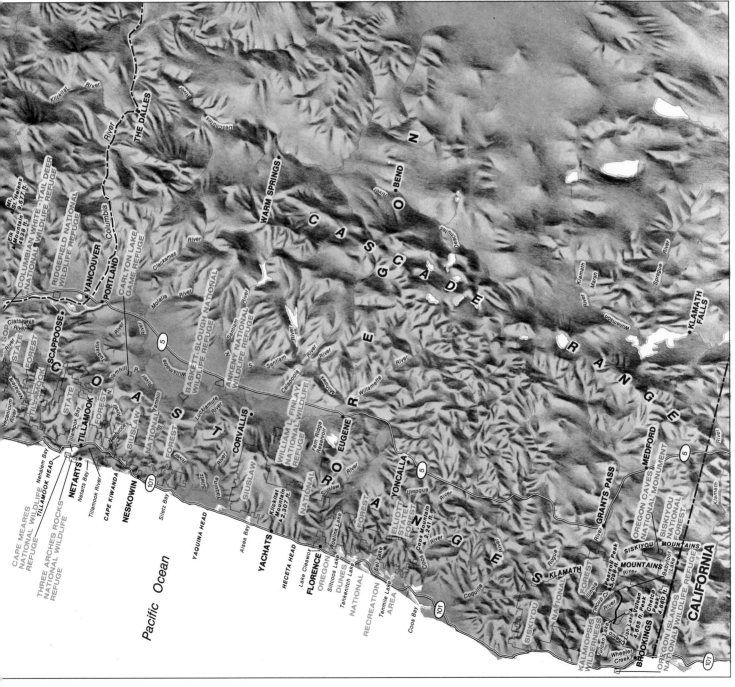

1/ A Land Defined by the Sea

The ocean heaves the weight of time ashore:
The rocks stand sheer.
White seafowl slowly skim immobile nests.

NELSON BENTLEY/ *SEA LION CAVES AND OTHER POEMS*

A lot of highway curves have been straightened out, and nearly all the Model Ts have gone rusting to the grave since I first drove up the Northwest coast in my venerable but valiant Ford. That was a generation ago. The old road followed the Oregon shoreline ever so faithfully, twisting and coiling along every cove and promontory, dodging the bigger rocks and trees, and hardly ever losing sight of the Pacific Ocean.

The Model T and I endured eight flat tires in one day of the bumpy, 1,000-mile homeward trip from San Francisco to Seattle. That didn't matter to me. It was springtime, and by daylight I could see the blue combers rolling in, screened occasionally as I drove past clumps of rhododendron with outrageously beautiful bursts of pink and purple blossoms. By moonlight the waves moved in majesty out of the mottled sea, flaunting long pale crests as they broke onto the sand. I knew there were pods of gray whales cruising offshore, and sometimes I saw the faint lights of coastwise ships. To my right were the dark foothills of the Siskiyous, and from time to time we rumbled over wooden bridges where wild rivers like the Rogue came roaring out of the mountains.

In the years since then I have homed in on the Northwest coast from every direction and by land, sea and air, but that old road from the south is still my favorite way to get there. Last year, with this book in mind, I drove it again to show five children a part of the country I had grown up in. We took my same route from San Francisco through the vineyards of the Napa Valley, because I wanted them to see the old winery town of Saint Helena, near where their great-grandparents had lived (and a generation before that, Robert Louis Stevenson and Jack London). I wanted them to breathe the head-clearing aroma of the tall, ever-peeling eucalyptus trees, a scent once smelled, never forgotten. Farther north we traveled the Redwood Highway, stopping in small, churchly groves of *Sequoia sempervirens* where the children stroked the rough bark of 300-foot-tall trees that have been reaching up for a thousand years and more to soak up the moisture of California's coastal fogs.

Across the state line, in Oregon, the coast highway has undergone lavish cosmetic surgery since my trip in the Model T. It has been broadened and gentled in grade and curvature to accommodate heavy traffic. Along with the traffic, an esthetic gas-station-and-hamburger-joint disaster has been visited on the roadside. But the blight is not inescapable. At the very edge of the sea, where by state law no tideland may be privately owned, the scene is pretty much pristine. There are still a hundred places where you can stop to climb a wave-washed rock, or roam the beach to listen to the surf and watch the gulls. Steller sea lions still inhabit their great caves near Florence, halfway up the coast. Offshore, at binocular range, the whales still come and go on their long migrations between the Arctic and their mating grounds at Scammon's Lagoon in Baja California. There are still places where you can get lost among 200-foot-high sand dunes that march inland along 50 miles of the coast, here and there engulfing stands of tall pines and cedars. And off to the east, in country too rugged for trailers, there still are the lonely Siskiyou and Siuslaw mountain forests to be tramped.

The magnificent Pacific seascape is the western boundary of the region this book will describe, a line where water and sky merge in an unbroken horizon formed by the curvature of the earth. The other limits of the Northwest coast depend on who does the defining. I have chosen as the northern limit the Nitinat Triangle, a fascinating wilderness area across the border in Canada on Vancouver Island; as the southern limit the Kalmiopsis Wilderness, an equally fascinating area that is enclosed by the Siskiyou National Forest in southwestern Oregon within sight of the California state line. Both the Nitinat and the Kalmiopsis are parts of the Coast Ranges, the mountain ramparts that rise right out of the sea all along western America, and both extend inland only a few miles. They are linked by about 500 miles of magnificent coastline, a dynamic meeting of earth and ocean that is the region's recurring theme.

Within the giant bracket formed by the Pacific, the Nitinat and the

Steller sea lions tend their pups on the rocks of an Oregon beach, sharing it with a flock of cormorants and a lone sea gull.

Kalmiopsis is the Olympic Peninsula in the state of Washington, heartland of the coastal wilderness. Until Alaska became a state the peninsula was the far corner of the United States. On three sides of it a narrow band of foothills descends steeply to salt water: the Pacific on the west, the Strait of Juan de Fuca (separating the United States and Canada) on the north and Puget Sound on the east. Its southern border, where the Olympic Range ends, is officially the Chehalis River, which empties into Grays Harbor midway on the Washington coast. But on a map or a satellite picture the great Columbia River, serving as the Washington-Oregon state line, seems a more natural boundary.

The Olympic Peninsula is an improbable physiographic assemblage of high-and-mighty mountain peaks, creeping glaciers, shadowy rain forests, brooding lakes, ferocious rivers and storm-battered shoreline. It remained pure wilderness for more than a century after the East Coast was tamed, and even now, in some of its fastnesses, it savages most human efforts to domesticate it.

The peninsula can be a perilous place where if you wander off a forest trail you may never be seen again; yet it is a romantic place where the sight of a delicate ice-age flower poking up through snow, or a 50-pound Chinook salmon hurtling rock falls to get upstream to spawn and die, can make you catch your breath in admiration for the tenacity of life. That tenacity applies to other creatures as well. The peninsula is the home of one of the densest populations of mountain lions, or cougars, anywhere in the world, and home also of the largest herd of Roosevelt elk, some 14,000 in all. Its offshore waters are a favorite abode of killer whales, which travel in packs, like wolves, and in seconds can gulp down anything that comes within range.

Sooner or later, walking along the shore, you make a discovery. You realize you are not merely on the western edge of America, but on the eastern edge of the Pacific Ocean. It is the sea before you, not the continent at your back, that has formed the character of the Northwest coast. It is this biggest of oceans that feeds the glaciers and the forests with rain, snow and fog, nurtures the rivers and lakes, carves away at the coastline and, periodically, has swallowed up the mountains and spewed them out again like broken teeth.

The Olympic Peninsula is now looped by a highway, a 325-mile extension of U.S. 101. On the day in the early 1930s when the last gap in this loop was to be closed, a ribbon-cutting ceremony was held on the ocean front at Kalaloch (klay-lock), a tiny Quinault Indian village where a forest stream pours through a tangle of driftwood logs onto a lovely sand beach. The *Seattle Times* considered this to be a golden-spike sort of event, marking the belated arrival of the automobile age in that country, and thus worthy of staff coverage. I was sent to cover it. The speechmaking was not memorable, but I recall a good deal of clam and salmon feasting, horn-tooting, whooping, hollering and Indian dancing.

The Quinaults would not have danced had they known what was in their future. For them the Olympic Loop Highway was to be more curse than blessing. Not only would it bring in motorists by the tens of thousands, but lumbermen and other invaders to chop up their forests and foul their air and water. But the beach at Kalaloch, at least, is now part of a 50-mile coastal corridor of Olympic National Park, and is protected within reason against casual pollution by passersby. It is still a joy to wander the shore, picking up pebbles and shells and bits of sand-polished wood. And there are reminders of the wild power of the elements. At times the tide may advance stealthily, posing mortal peril to the walker in the shape of great driftwood logs suddenly set in juggernaut motion by the rising water.

What keeps so much of the Olympic Peninsula wild is that at no point is it penetrated more than a few miles by the stub roads leading off U.S. 101. At the most, these dead-end roads afford only a peek at the wilderness within. Some townspeople around the perimeter keep lobbying for crisscrossing highways and skyrides that would enable visitors on wheels to reach the interior that is now reachable only by arduous foot and horse trails. Fortunately, neither the National Park Service nor the Forest Service—which between them control the bulk of the peninsula—has the money or strong desire for such Disneyland-type projects. They have kept things simple, and there are no imposing lodges in the Olympic Mountains like those in Yellowstone.

The Park Service, under the Department of the Interior, manages Olympic National Park, about 900,000 acres of hard-core wilderness in the middle of the peninsula, plus a thin ocean strip to the west. Throughout the park logging is prohibited, and so are firearms and hunting; but fishing is permitted. The Forest Service, under the Department of Agriculture, is in charge of the Olympic National Forest, 700,000 acres that all but surround the park. The Park Service is dedicated solely to conservation; the Forest Service has a multiplicity of responsibilities —for recreational use of its lands, conservation of scenic areas, range management, mining, watershed protection, fire prevention—but one of its major activities is selling timber to loggers.

Both agencies employ polite rangers in flat-brimmed Smokey-Bear hats, and both maintain trails and shelters for public use. But in a sense the two operate at cross purposes. The landscape testifies to this: the park is unscalped and green everywhere, while the forest is checkerboarded with close-cropped tracts without a single tree. The conflict of interest has increasingly troubled the entire Pacific Northwest. For many years Washington and Oregon, along with British Columbia, have been America's main source of softwood lumber. But today tourism has begun to rival timber as a revenue-producer in the region, and tourists do not come to see the approximately 50 per cent of the Olympic National Forest that has been cut over, selectively and otherwise. The fact that you cannot eat your wilderness and have it is not easy for the Northwest—or the nation—to face.

There is no way to experience the entire Northwest coast in a weekend or a month, and there is no central point from which to explore it, short of setting up headquarters on a mountaintop. I wanted to walk the beaches, penetrate the forests, get up among the glaciers, and revisit various lakes and rivers, and I also wanted my family to share some of these experiences. After due reconnaissance I found an ideal base, a 70-year-old log house on Hood Canal, in the lee of the Olympics and in striking distance of everywhere I wanted to go.

Hood Canal is a narrow 70-mile-long arm of Puget Sound, sculpted by Pleistocene glaciers, with a crook in the elbow that is called The Great Bend. It was explored by Captain George Vancouver by longboat in 1792. He wanted to see if it led anywhere, which it did not, and he named it for a British naval dignitary, who never laid eyes on it.

Our log house looked west across The Great Bend at a point where the canal is about two miles wide. The place came with tall firs and cedars, salmonberry and blackberry bushes, fallen alder from nearby woods to stoke the big stone fireplace, and a hundred feet of pebbly beach. The beach in turn came with little butter clams, which could be dug at low tide, and with big Pacific oysters, which did not even have to be dug because they lie right there among the pebbles. Oysters can survive many hours of being stranded on the shore by the tide; their oxygen requirements are low, and a powerful muscle enables them to keep their shells tightly closed against dehydration.

In Hood Canal, more than 100 miles from the Pacific via Puget Sound and the Strait of Juan de Fuca, the water exchanges itself only four times a year, simply because it has so far to go on an ebb tide that the incoming tide turns it around before it can go all the way out. It is nonetheless clean enough for the oysters to thrive in. The scavenging gulls help keep it that way, and so do the voracious and carnivorous Dungeness and rock crabs, which patrol the bottom well below the low-tide zone. The crabs were even better eating than the baby clams or oysters. Our crab pot often held half a dozen of them, big and squirming, when we rowed out to check on it. Mindful of state law, we kept only the males, whose triangular plate on the underside of the body is slender where the female's is wide, and we threw back anything less than six inches across the body.

The road that winds around Hood Canal, in back of houses like ours, is lined with evergreen trees and an occasional crooked-limbed, red-barked madroña. Like the canal itself, the road quiets down in September. In that month a cool fog hangs over the water in the mornings, and when it burns off there are red and russet patches among the second-growth evergreens on the far shore—the vine maples putting on their autumn dress. The waves lap the beach, the gulls cry to one another, and every few minutes there is a loud smack as a salmon jumps out of the water and slams back. Just once, at dusk, we saw a spaniel's head with cat's whiskers poke above the still surface. It was a harbor seal, fishing for dinner many miles from its ocean home. It stared at us from a safe distance out, then submerged. Moments later it reappeared a hundred yards away for another look, then disappeared for good.

A few miles west of The Great Bend, seeming to rise straight out of the woods, is part of the snowy skyline of the Olympic Mountains. Hourly its coloration changes—from austere grays and browns to extravagant sunset shades of orange and lavender—but its saw-toothed façade is always dominated by Mount Ellinor and Mount Washington. If you look their way and tilt your head to the right you can make out a recumbent George Washington's profile, as plain as on the 25-cent coin. When his every feature is sharp and unclouded in the evening sky, so it is said, tomorrow is sure to be a fine day.

On a balmy afternoon or starry night the mountains appear calm and approachable, with no hint of danger in their aspect. That is an illusion. While neither hostile nor friendly, this wilderness is a place where you cannot be too careful—as I was reminded, forcibly and agonizingly, shortly after we had moved into the log house. On a bright Friday in July, I drove my sons Richard, David and Robert, with Henry Perez, an older and experienced hiking companion, to the starting point

Hood Canal, a salt-water arm of Puget Sound,

shimmers in the afternoon sun. Across the canal, the Olympic Mountains begin abruptly and stretch westward, rising above 6,000 feet.

of an overnight camping trip. We rounded Lake Cushman, just below Ellinor and Washington, and passed the ranger station called Staircase,
after a series of falls on the Skokomish River. The trailhead was at the
end of a punishing road a few miles farther into the mountains and
well inside Olympic National Park. At 2 o'clock we synchronized our
watches and agreed that I would pick the boys up 26 hours later, on
their return from either Flapjack lakes or Black and White lakes, which
they had pinpointed on their topographical map.

At 4 o'clock the next afternoon I was back at the trailhead, deep in
the quiet woods. No one came or went. At 6 o'clock I drove down to
Staircase Station to talk with Floyd Dickerson, a young ranger. He wanted to know if the boys were competent hikers, which they were, and
how much food they had taken along, which was plenty for four meals.
"They won't starve," he said, "but let's hope they don't freeze—it
snowed four inches last night at the 5,000-foot level. A lot of the trails
are probably obliterated; and anyway, it will be dark soon. I think you
should come back in the morning and we'll see how things look."

I was back in the morning, with my wife, and things did not look
good: there had been more snow and clouds covered most of the sky.

"Why don't I just hike in and look for them?" I asked Floyd.

"Too many trails to cover up there. Better we get organized." So we
waited, while radio messages went back and forth between Staircase
and Station 730, the park headquarters far to the north at Port Angeles.
The radio worked only fitfully, because atmospheric conditions were
bad and because Staircase sits in a pocket of mountains where signals
are often blocked off. After a while Mary and I walked across a bridge
over the Skokomish to an army tent occupied by Beren Harrington, a
ranger naturalist, and his wife. We shared their coffee and walked back
to the station. The hours passed. A search party was coming, and meanwhile Beren and Floyd went about moving the ranger-station flagpole
across a roadway and stepping it in a hole near the front door.

Late in the afternoon the sky brightened a bit and Staircase asked
730, "How about getting a helicopter in here while there's still some
daylight?" The answer was no, not just now; the only available chopper was busy up the Dosewallips road, four valleys to the north. It was
looking for a tourist who had stepped out of his car to take a picture of
the spectacular "Dosey" falls. There had been nothing to step onto, and
he had plunged into the river, some 200 feet down.

Then a pair of hikers came by and reported that up on a trail they
had heard calls for help from the other side of the Skokomish gorge.

Beren grabbed a hand radio from the porch steps, jumped into a Park Service panel truck and took off. Less than an hour later the search party, mobilized by park headquarters, set out in his wake. It included three carloads of volunteers from Search Dogs of Washington, who had brought along four German shepherds and two bloodhounds, and ranger Jack Hughes, who had driven 100 miles from his own station at Lake Crescent and who knew the Skokomish high country by heart.

They were on the road, ready to fan out on the trails when Beren came on his radio. "Eight three oh," he called, "this is Harrington. Found the boys and they're all okay; we'll be down to the road shortly."

They were tired, hungry and dirty, but safe; and before long they were back at Staircase, piling out of one of the Search Dog trucks, along with two of the German shepherds. Yes, Henry Perez told us, it had snowed up where they were, "and then it got foggy, sort of a white-out where you couldn't tell up from down. The trail just petered out."

"They did the right thing," Beren said. "They headed for a clearing and stayed put, instead of wandering. You kids shouldn't feel bad about this—it could happen to anybody, even rangers."

We thanked everybody concerned and loaded the boys into the car for the trip back to Hood Canal. I stopped in at the little ranger station to say goodbye to the burly new head ranger, George Bowen, who had just been transferred from Kings Canyon Park in California and was having a busy first weekend on the job. "I know you've been worried," he said. "But as you know, it could have been much worse. I just heard from the people in the chopper up the Dosewallips. They found the body of the man who stepped out of his car."

Well, it is not a point to labor. Stepping off a curb can be dangerous, too, if an accident is waiting to happen. The Olympics looked no more menacing the next morning than they had before. The clouds had gone, and the mountains looked clear, serene, inviting. I had risen at day-break to get ready for a hike of my own that was to start three hours later and 150 miles away on the far side of the Olympic Range. It promised to be a good day to set out on a 44-mile backpacking trip. I glanced in at the boys, safely sleeping in their beds, and started off.

A Shore under Siege

PHOTOGRAPHS BY HARALD SUND

The 500 miles of Pacific coastline from the Strait of Juan de Fuca south to the Oregon-California border is a thunderous battleground where sea and land meet in stark confrontation. There are no offshore barrier reefs or island groups to buffer the shock of waves that have been wind-driven across the longest stretch of open ocean in the Northern Hemisphere—6,000 miles from Japan.

As a result, the Northwest coast experiences some of the most violent surf anywhere. Normal winter storms pound the shore with 20-foot waves that break against coastal cliffs with a shock that is roughly equivalent to the impact of a car gunned into a stone wall at 90 miles per hour. Vivid evidence of the ferocity with which these waves can strike is provided by a steel grating across the beacon atop Tillamook Head lighthouse, a tower that rises 139 feet from a rock off the Oregon coast; the grating had to be installed to protect the beacon's glass from rocks thrown at it by capricious waves. In a December storm around the turn of the century, a 135-pound rock was catapulted more than 100 feet into the air, then fell and smashed a hole 20 feet square in the roof of the lightkeeper's house

and practically gutted the interior.

Aside from such spectacular demonstrations, the sea's most effective tactic against the land is ceaseless attrition. About every 10 seconds in interminable repetition, small waves break on the shore and work to wear it down with stones and coarse sand they pick up from the sea bottom. In time cliffs are ground into beaches, forests are eaten away, headlands are destroyed. As the sea attacks, it captures further weapons from the adversary: the undermined rocks and trees that fall into the surf are picked up and used as the tools for further assaults on the coast.

Where the coast is relatively unyielding, the sea's success against the land is measured in minute amounts and long time spans—it may take thousands of years to wear down a pillar of basalt. But where the coast is not so rock bound, it is more vulnerable and the destruction can be dramatic: at Cape Shoalwater, on the Washington coast, the sea has chewed away as much as 200 feet of the sandy shore in one year. Here, as at Tillamook Head, the waves have little regard for man's work: the lighthouse at the cape has been moved back three times in little more than a century.

A train of frothy, sediment-laden waves, seen from above, carries the tools of erosion to the job of grinding the shoreline. In one day ocean currents can bring 1,000 tons of erosive material to bear on one mile of coast.

Grinding waves scallop the shore and litter it with huge logs.

The Tools of Demolition

The erosion process that wears down the Northwest coast employs an array of powerful tools. The most effective by far are the waves themselves and the loads of sediment they carry with them as they smash the shore, pummeling it with every surge. The grinding and wearing effect takes many years to produce noticeable results, but its force is relentless and inexorable.

Sometimes the process scoops out a series of crescent-shaped beaches *(left)*. In the case of the sea stacks pictured at right, an unseen force also plays a decisive role. Air, trapped and rammed by the water into natural cracks in the stacks, builds up pressures so terrific that they actually cause the rock to explode. Individual detonations are usually invisible, but the cumulative effect of a series of such explosions may be to detach chunks of rock weighing tons and send them crashing into the sea.

The land itself supplies an instrument of its destruction, in the form of enormous trees from the adjacent forests that have fallen victim to the sea and lie strewn about the beaches of the Northwest coast. On calm days, as seen at left, these great hulks lie immovable, 8 to 10 deep at the high-water mark, like giants' whitened bones. But when the sea rises, driven by storms or high tides *(overleaf)*, the logs are picked up, swept out to sea and then hurled back at the coast like battering rams.

Deceptively ethereal, ocean spray bursts against offshore chunks of sandstone that will someday fall to the sea's endless onslaught.

A flotilla of logs, launched by an unusually high tide, menaces a stretch of Washington shoreline. Some of them measuring 35 feet long, these formidable weapons can inflict severe damage. In time the battered shore will be worn away, and the pine tree standing at right will topple into the water to become, like the others, a derelict—and a potential weapon.

The color and texture of a mineral-streaked boulder show its origin—the base of the cliff (background) from which it was torn by the sea.

The Destruction of a Cliff

The Northwest coast is one of the most precipitous in the world, and where its steep cliffs rise from the ocean with no shelving beach for protection, the result is a devastating encounter. Pounding against the cliffsides and surging repeatedly into opened crevices, the waves gouge out the base and bring the overhanging rock crashing down, a process called undercutting.

The boulder in the foreground at left is the remnant of just such an attack on the cliff behind it. Having toppled the boulder, the waves are gradually moving it seaward and wearing it down into smaller pieces —ammunition for further attack on the cliff. A severe storm could even pick up the whole rock and fling it at the cliff base. Waves have moved eight-ton rocks as much as 70 feet.

Another result of undercutting is the creation of outlets for fresh ground water that seeps out of a newly sliced cliff. In the picture at right the reddish-brown colors at the center of the cliff face are caused by minerals carried in the water that oozes out of cracks and pores in the exposed rocks. The water spurting from the top of the cliff marks the site of two tiny brooks that were converted into a small waterfall when the cliff was undercut.

In winter the ground water that oozes through the cutaway cliffside freezes, thus enlarging the cracks in the rocks and further hastening the process of erosion.

Mineral-rich ground water stains a cliff undercut by the sea.

The Slow Birth of a Beach

Amidst the rocky ledges, cobbles and pebbles cluttering this stretch of the Washington coast, a beach is being born. Its creation actually began about 4,000 years ago, when the sea, fed by melting glaciers, rose to its present level and immediately set to hammering at the shore. Cliffs were gouged, undercut and eventually ground down so that nothing now remains but rocky washboard ridges. These too are being rasped down by the abrasive rocks and pebbles they have yielded to the waves.

As the process goes on, the ledges will be further reduced until they form a submerged rocky platform —the basement of a beach. The sea itself will play a vital part in the final steps of beach-building. While tearing down, it is also building up. Some debris is already being deposited on the rock ledge and as time passes the particles will be ground finer. Eventually the sea will bring in sand and leave it on the platform. At first the sand will be only a thin coating that can be blown or washed away by winter storms. But within a few centuries or even sooner, a true beach will have been created—narrow and limited in extent, bounded by rocky headlands and sheer cliffs like many on the Northwest coast, but covered with deep, soft sand. The rocks and ledges pictured here will be gone, but the sea will find other cliffs, other boulders to challenge in its ceaseless war against the coast (overleaf).

Rippled by centuries of scouring, layered sandstone ledges lie exposed to the wave erosion

that will further transform them into a sandy beach. The layers, once horizontal, were tilted by upheavals in the earth 30 million years ago.

Carved from a cliff, these massive boulders are evidence of the sea's persistent sculpting, a process seen in miniature in the rocky bowl in

the foreground. Here at each high tide waves spin small rocks around, their abrasive movements widening and deepening the hollow.

2/ The Icy Road to Olympus

*The mountains seem to rise from the edge of the
water…as though nature had designed to shut up this
spot for her safe retreat forever.*

EUGENE SEMPLE, GOVERNOR OF WASHINGTON TERRITORY/ *FROM THE SEATTLE PRESS, 1888*

It is a sunny midsummer afternoon and we are hiking up the icy north
flank of Mount Olympus. The long valley of the Hoh River rain forest
is well behind us and thousands of feet below. At our backs is the
broad expanse of Blue Glacier, biggest of the seven glaciers that adorn
Olympus. Not far ahead rises the mountain's summit, the highest point
in the Olympic Range, and on one of its shoulders perches a glacier-
research station, which is our destination. We know the mountaintop is
there because earlier in our climb we saw its multiple peaks of rock silhouetted emphatically against a pale blue sky. But it has been out of
our sight for an hour now, blocked from view by the steep 40° slope
of the Snow Dome, a 1,100-foot-high mound of ice and compacted
snow piled on a rock foundation at the edge of the Blue Glacier.

Nine people are toiling up Snow Dome's white wall, roped together
in threes. The lead group has already vanished over the crest of the
dome, and the second group is a few yards ahead of us. For my own
bone-tired threesome—park ranger Bill Ferraro, his wife Joan and me,
spaced out by 50-foot lengths of rope—the climbing rhythm is fune-
really slow, five steps worth of rest for every five steps upward. We dig
in carefully at every step, for the snow is slippery even under our crampons and ice axes. Perhaps it is ridiculous that we should be panting so
hard. After all, this isn't Mount Everest, or even the 9,550-foot original
Greek version of Olympus, but only its 7,976-foot American namesake.

Nevertheless at 6,000 feet plus, and unaccustomed to this straight-up kind of climbing, we are panting, bent over our ice axes, glad to get breath any way we can.

From the head end of our rope Bill Ferraro calls down cheerfully to Joan and me, "Honest, it's just a little farther to the top," and sure enough in 15 minutes the Snow Dome levels off at last and Olympus re-appears to our left, its peaks hardly a thousand feet farther up. A quarter of a mile ahead and a little downgrade we see two prefab huts, anchored to a rock shelf in the shelter of a lesser peak. This is the University of Washington's glacier-research station, and its lean and bearded chief glaciologist, Dr. Edward LaChapelle, is waiting at his door with a smile and a big kettle of boiling-hot tea. "You're probably ready for this," he says. We hunker down and sip his tea gratefully, staring out at the thin, drifting clouds that repeatedly veil and unveil the mountain in white and sunset pink.

At twilight, feeling rested, we clamber up the rise behind the huts and see at once why it is known informally as Panic Peak: standing on its crumbly pinnacle you are one step away from a 2,000-foot precipice.

For our benefit, LaChapelle sets up his theodolite, a surveying instrument used to measure angles and distant elevations. Through its telescopic sight we take turns peering at Jupiter and three of its moons, suspended over Olympus in the southern sky, and at the earth's own moon—orange, crescent shaped and hanging low in the west. A light blinks below it—the Destruction Island lighthouse, out in the Pacific perhaps some 40 miles from where we stand. A vague breeze is blowing from that direction, cooled along the way by the White Glacier, which drops down dizzyingly into the darkness at our feet. In another month this same wind off the ocean, no longer so faint, will bring the first flakes of the winter's scores of feet of snow. It was from somewhere out there, when he sailed past in 1788, that the English navigator Captain John Meares caught sight of the mountain we are standing on and named it Olympus, thinking it beautiful and grand enough to be a dwelling place of the gods.

The next morning there is a crust of ice on our sleeping bags and tarpaulins, bright blobs of blue and orange spread out on the brown rocks of Panic Peak. The stars and moon are gone but the top of Olympus is in lordly view, standing bold and clear over the Snow Dome's crest. Actually, it has not one peak but several—East, Middle and West, the highest. A subordinate peak is known as False Summit because half a century ago a pioneering party of amateur climbers scaled it, thinking they were gaining the ultimate top, only to look westward and realize that the mountain had one more, slightly higher spire.

Olympus is one of 35 mountains in the Olympic Range that rise 7,000 feet or more, and there are hundreds of other, smaller ones, many of them unnamed, that thrust up helter-skelter from the deeply dissected valleys and canyons of the Olympic Peninsula. The first impression one gets of the mountains when surveying them from such a lofty vantage as the Snow Dome is that of an undecipherable jumble. There are no orderly ranks of summits, no parallel ranges, no groups of solitary, majestic spires. Just a welter of rocky peaks and icy ridges scattered about as though the choppy waves of a storm-blown sea had been frozen in their confusion.

Looking at the mountains' disorder, I was not surprised to learn that the geological events that formed the Olympics in the first place are somewhat jumbled as well. Geologists have a hard time piecing together all the puzzles posed by the mountains' battered rocks. One thing is clear: the Olympics were not produced by volcanic eruptions, as were so many of the Cascade Mountains only 100 miles to the east. They are, rather, the wreckage of an underseas collision between two sections of the earth's crust, thickly layered with sedimentary rock. The confrontation forced one section down and, under great compression, its layers of sediment were scraped by the edge of the other section into a confused heap. The resulting pile of cracked, twisted rocks was thrust thousands of feet above the surface—and thus the original Olympics were formed. But they were to be worn down by erosion, covered by the sea and turbulently raised up again at least two more times, maybe three, in a process that took 65 million years and eventually produced the Olympics in their present mass.

Since they came essentially from the sea floor, most of the mountains' rocks are or once were sedimentary—shale, siltstone and sandstone that built up as layers of sand and mud thousands of feet thick. Heat and pressure over the eons metamorphosed some of the rock into fine-grained slate and coarser phyllite. There is also a lot of volcanic rock, such as the bulging cliff of "pillow lava" near Dosewallips Falls not far from Hood Canal. But that lava did not erupt from volcanoes; it was extruded from seams onto the ocean floor where it quickly cooled into piled-up pillow shapes, like hot taffy in cold water. Later it was lifted in a jumble with the sedimentary material whose horizontal layers were so bent and folded that they now lie at all angles.

The rock that was thus battered and eroded understandably has a tortured look. In many places, as in the peaks of Mount Olympus itself, it is cracked and rotten enough to crumble underfoot. Elsewhere, slate lies on the surface like piles of broken glass, its shards sharp enough to cut the toughest hiking boot. Part of this deterioration can be credited to the other great shaping force in the mountains' geologic past—ice. At least four times in the Pleistocene epoch that ended 10,000 years ago, ice inched down from the north to cover the Olympics so that all but the highest peaks were engulfed. Along the way these arctic glaciers dug out Puget Sound and the Strait of Juan de Fuca, and gouged into the canyons and ravines of the mountains. (The only granite to be found in the Olympics, at elevations up to 3,500 feet, is in the form of huge boulders that were carted down by the northern ice and then left behind like castoff baubles when the ice retreated.) Between the great ice ages and since their end, smaller glaciers born on the mountains themselves have gouged down the same ravines, making flat- or round-bottomed canyons out of V-shaped ones. These individual, or alpine, glaciers are still very much alive in the Olympics, and their gleaming icefields are one of the mountains' most noticeable features.

Nature, of course, is still performing minor surgery on the mountains, slowly altering their features with wind and ice erosion, avalanches and rockslides. All these operations, past and present, have combined to give the Olympics the very rugged profile that presents itself to a hiker looking out from Mount Olympus.

A somewhat different profile appears if you look at the Olympics from sea level. From the east and the north, particularly from Hood Canal or the Strait of Juan de Fuca, the mountains rise abruptly from the very edge of the land and pile up to imposing heights—an inscrutable wall that gives no clue of what is beyond, except for a few jutting peaks.

At 7,976 feet, the highest altitude in the Olympics is not so imposing compared with the continent's tallest ranges, but the abruptness of their elevation is. The Olympics tower to as great a height over the sea as most of the Rockies do above the western Plains. Yet, because of their proximity to the sea (no place in the range is more than 30 miles from salt water), the Olympics tend to look taller than they are, an illusion heightened by the fog and mist that often swathe the peaks. This ethereal shroud also lends an air of mystery to the mountains that was powerfully felt by the Indians and first white settlers. I can attest that it is still effective, although the range has been pretty well explored.

Given the rugged nature and mysterious aura of the Olympics, it is easy to understand that they were considered a formidable and unapproachable fastness until modern times. The coastal Indians, though they lived on the lower fringes of this wild high country, rarely ventured far up into it. Its elk and deer wintered in the lowlands, where the animals could easily be killed—and besides, the Indians' legends told them all they wanted to know about the interior. They believed the outer wall of the mountains, rising sharply from sea level, guarded a lush and lovely valley, green and serene as a Himalayan Shangri-la —except that it was the dwelling place of the dread Thunder Bird and therefore a place for people to avoid. Indians of many tribes have a variety of myths about a great bird that causes thunder, but the coastal tribes were quite specific about the creature. James G. Swan, an amateur anthropologist who lived among them in the 1850s, recorded various names for the immense bird whose outstretched wings could obscure the heavens. It was *Hah-ness* to the Chinook, *Thlew-cloots* to the Makah, *Too-tootsh* or *Tatooche* to the Nootka. Tucked under its wing it kept a giant sea horse, called *Hah-hake-to-ak* by the Makah, useful for killing whales and loosing lightning bolts.

The Seattle Press expeditionaries of 1890, first to cross the Olympic Peninsula, mark their adventure a few hours after its finish by having a studio portrait made, complete with one of their dogs. Their trek through the mountain wilds took 22 weeks and exposed them to extreme cold, near-starvation and other perils, but they achieved their aim, which team leader James Christie (second from right) said was to solve "the mystery lying at the very door of Seattle."

This Thunder Bird, Swan reported, "is an Indian of gigantic proportions, who lives on top of the mountains. His food is whales, and when hungry he puts on his wings and feathers as an Indian wraps himself in a blanket, and sails out in search of his prey. When a whale is discovered, the *Hah-hake-to-ak* darts out its fiery tongue, which kills the fish; and as the mighty bird settles down to seize it in its talons, the rustling of its great wings produces the thunder. The whale, when seized, is taken up into the mountain and devoured."

The white man did not credit those tales; nevertheless it took him an uncommonly long time to get up into the maze of mountains and see for himself what was there. Most people were content to look at them from below, and the adventurous few who were not were turned back by rough weather and tough terrain before penetrating much deeper than the foothills. As late as 1889, when most of the farthest reaches of America had been explored and mapped, no human being had ever entered the Olympic Peninsula on one side and emerged on the other. (At least, no one could prove that he had.) As a reporter for the Seattle *Press* wrote in 1889, "Washington has her great unknown land like the interior of Africa." And Elisha P. Ferry, the first governor of Washington after it became the 42nd state that same year, suggested in an interview that there was a fine opportunity for someone "to acquire fame by unveiling the mystery which wraps the land encircled by the snow-capped Olympic range."

That was all the encouragement that Edmond S. Meany, a zealous 27-year-old staff member of the *Press,* needed. Meany organized a meeting between the paper's owner and a group of explorers, and in the first week of December 1889, a six-man "Press Exploring Expedition" was on its way. (The group was soon reduced to five when one man returned to Seattle because his wife had become ill.) The leader of the expedition was a former Indian fighter and Canadian Arctic explorer, James H. Christie; its topographer was Charles A. Barnes, a onetime captain in the U.S. Revenue Marine who claimed a great deal of mountaineering experience. They took along four dogs, plenty of rifles and ammunition and 1,500 pounds of other gear, plus 50 pounds of "colored fire" (probably the powder used in fireworks) to burn on a high peak on an appointed night when Meany would be watching in Seattle.

But they were also burdened with bad luck and bad judgment. At Port Angeles on the north shore of the peninsula, they decided to head up the nearby Elwha River by boat, thinking it would be the fastest way to transport their supplies, and hoping that from its headwaters they would find a route to take them out of the mountains. So they spent a month building a flatboat, without ever reconnoitering the El- wha to see if it was navigable. It was not. An angry little river full of boiling rapids and sheer-walled canyons, the Elwha fought the men at every turn, and after 10 drenched days of pulling, hauling and falling into it, they abandoned their boat. They next built sledges, but these bogged down in the wet dead-of-winter snow. They recruited two mules, but one fell down a cliff and the other became so exhausted they turned her loose. From then on it was backpacking all the way, fer- rying supplies a mile or so and going back for more.

Today you can see the valley of the Elwha from the safe vantage point of Hurricane Ridge, a lookout promontory inland and upland from Port Angeles. The valley twists and turns for a long way through the for- ested hills, then rounds a corner and vanishes somewhere in the confusion of distant mountains. To the *Press* party, the valley must have seemed without end. After more than 100 days they still had not put the headwaters of the river behind them. Their food dwindled; time after time they were saved from starvation by a lucky shot at a bear, deer or elk. Their 50 pounds of "colored fire" they kicked down- hill one day in disgust, realizing there were too many hills between them and Seattle for it to be visible there anyway.

They were not really lost, for they knew that if they pressed south far enough they would find a river that flowed south or west to lead them out toward the Pacific. But they were often confused and in that lofty labyrinth kept mistaking one peak or divide or stream for another. What they called Mount Bennett was really Olympus; and what they believed to be Olympus was really another group of peaks. Finally, as they had hoped, but only after 14 weeks of hard climbing, they did find a route to the southwest by crossing a divide and descending a river, where they eventually encountered a white hunter and his Indian guides. In a roomy canoe, the Indians paddled them down to Lake Quinault. After what they had been through, they had no trouble with the 40-mile trip from there to the Pacific, and thence down the beach to the city of Ab- erdeen on the Chehalis River at the peninsula's southern edge. They had set out in December, it was now May.

So the Olympics were traversed at last. No verdant grassy valley lay up there, let alone the nest of the Thunder Bird, but at least the ex- plorers showed that it was possible to cross the peninsula and come

Mountain goats rummage for moss and grass beneath the snow of Olympic National Park's Mount Angeles. These rare natives of the high slopes are easily alarmed and can vanish with remarkable sure-footedness into the rockiest, most inaccessible terrain.

out alive, even if it did take six months. Behind them they left a rudely blazed trail, and they conferred names on more than 50 peaks and rivers that had never been on a map before under any name—because there had been no map. Press lords like Joseph Pulitzer and James Gordon Bennett had mountains named for them, and so did the city of Seattle. Nor did the explorers neglect to name landmarks after themselves, including Mount Christie and Mount Barnes. Many decades later I knew the enterprising young newspaperman who had promoted their expedition, but knew him as a venerable and revered professor of history at the University of Washington. He was tall and goateed and carried himself with dignity and grace, as was fitting, for he too had a mountain in the Olympics named after him: Mount Meany, 6,695 feet.

The mountains are no less rugged now than when the *Press* expedition struggled through them, but in places the going has been made easier. Our trip up Mount Olympus, which ended with Ed LaChapelle's cup of tea, had begun a day and a half earlier on a pleasant trail leading east and up from the Hoh River Ranger Station. It led through the dimly lit rain forest where spruce, red cedar and hemlock gradually gave way, as we gained altitude, to stands of silver fir and then subalpine fir. We camped the first night at Elk Lake, a dark-blue mountain gem 14 miles out from the ranger station. In the morning Bill Ferraro cached all the food and equipment we would not need until our return, stringing a heavy sack between two trees 10 feet in the air, out of the reach of bears. Then we killed our fire and headed up the trail. In a few minutes Elk Lake vanished into the trees.

A couple of miles on we passed Glacier Meadows, which at 4,100 feet are about 1,600 feet higher than Elk Lake. Here the vegetation thins out to stunted subalpine fir only six to eight feet tall, Sitka alder and scrubby salmonberry bushes. The meadows are inaptly named; they are just a break in the woods with two rustic shelters that show signs of heavy use (meaning tin cans and other litter) because many hikers camp here and go no farther, and neglect to "pack it out." But little Jemrod Creek, flowing a few yards away, is clean and cold, and away from the shelters there was no sign of man. It is in places like this, near timberline, that the Olympic marmot is likely to be found—or at least heard. The marmot is a large member of the squirrel family, and the most interesting thing about it is the high-pitched whistle that it sounds at the approach of danger. And indeed, as we advanced, a whistle came; but the marmot, with no way of knowing our benign intentions, remained warily out of sight.

Its colors blending with its timberline habitat, an Olympic marmot sits up to survey the surroundings. This large alpine rodent is more often heard than seen. Its shrill whistle at the hint of any danger makes it an unwitting scout for hunted creatures, and at times a galling tattletale for hunters.

Above the meadows and above treeline, which is at 5,000 feet, we checked ourselves out on crampons and ice axes as a safety precaution before assailing, in turn, the Blue Glacier and the Snow Dome. Our practice slope was a small north-facing snowfield, shaped like a bisected ice-cream cone, bulging over a rockslide we had just surmounted by scrambling up it from the meadows on all fours. The snowfield was so steeply curved that from the top we could not see the talus, or jumbled rock, at the bottom. The trick we had to master was to run, not walk, downhill on the snow until we could no longer stay upright, then somehow to belly flop and with both hands plunge the sharp pick of the ax into the snow to stop our descent, meanwhile keeping legs spread apart and back arched up to provide a three-point braking action. (All this, of course, to minimize the danger in case of a real fall when we climbed the Snow Dome.) We all mastered the maneuver more or less awkwardly; once you caught on, in fact, it was fun.

Crampons are not much good on rock, so we strapped them onto our packs before picking our way over the rocky moraine that lay between our practice snowfield and the Blue Glacier itself. There is no trail across this treacherous, boulder-strewn barrier, but here and there a little pile of stones serves as a road sign showing where other climbers have passed. We clambered down the lichen-stained rocks on the far side of the moraine to nibble a trail lunch of dried beef and candy bars and took a good long look at the fantastic vista before us.

The glacier sloped gently up to our left; above it, past the head of the broad, sweeping curve of ice, was the grand massif of Mount Olympus, a line of bare crags jutting above capes of ermine-white snow. In the clear air and intense white light of the heights, it looked deceptively close. In the middle distance, the glacier gleamed brightly, a field of white shot here and there with flashes of the pure hue responsible for its name. (The show of color comes from the icy walls of the glacier's chasms and crevasses, which absorb the longer wave lengths of light and reflect the shorter blue waves.) Directly in front of us the glacier surface was neither white nor blue but tattletale gray, littered with pebbles and other natural debris. It was also humming with the combined gurgles of subsurface rivulets, the meltwater of snowstorms past, bearing downslope the fine debris of decades and making the immense river of ice seem alive and pulsing.

Miles off to our right, the far side of the rain-forest valley we had traversed was a curtain of dark green. Above and beyond it rose more peaks, cradling the snow-patched alpine meadows called Cat Basin, a summer home of the Roosevelt elk. Some of the timbered slopes in this panorama were streaked with brighter green, chutes where new undergrowth was taking hold in the wake of old snowslides. Earlier in the day, picking our way over the debris left by a recent slide, someone had caught a faint flicker of movement out of the corner of an eye and we had looked up—almost straight up—and had seen something moving a couple of thousand feet closer to the sky. It was a mountain goat, a tiny blur of off-white against the blinding snow. Introduced half a century ago to these mountains, where they had never lived before, the goats made themselves at home and in a vigorous copulation explosion have increased in number from less than a dozen to more than 300.

But now no goat or bird or bush but only ice and snow and rock were in view ahead. We applied sunburn cream, strapped on the crampons and roped ourselves together for the trip across the glacier. The ropes —7/16-inch nylon that will not break with a 4,000-pound jerk—seemed a bit ostentatious, but they are cheap insurance in such a place: if one falls, there are two to help. We prudently trudged around the crevasses that were three feet or more across, but even in hopping a deep two-foot crack, it was good to know that a slip need not bring instant interment in a sandwich of ice. We crossed the glacier diagonally, skirting the ends of six-foot-wide crevasses that looked to be 100 feet deep. A fresh snowfall had left their lips white and softly rounded, but when you peered down into them, the color of their sheer walls turned from pale aqua to intense turquoise.

Between crevasses the snow was crustless, like soft beach sand or a field of sugar, and seemingly bottomless, but the crampons gave us good, crunchy traction. Our route was slightly uphill and we walked slowly, pausing while Bill figured the best way around a crevasse or a shadow in the surface that might cloak an unopened crevasse. Forty minutes of this careful, evasive navigating brought us to the base of the towering ice fall that descends on both sides of a rock outcropping to feed the glacier. The ice fall, more than 1,000 feet high and studded with white-and-blue blocks of ice as big as houses, is unclimbable. The way up the mountain dodges around it to the right—up another tributary of the glacier, the great swelling breast of the Snow Dome. And so, after our slow and for me painful ascent of the dome, we came finally and gratefully to Ed LaChapelle's eyrie.

Glaciologists have figured out that about three quarters of the world's supply of fresh water is contained in the ice that now covers a tenth of the earth's land masses. More than 97 per cent of this water is held in two of the planet's frozen assets, the Greenland and Antarctic ice sheets. Not much of the remaining 3 per cent is in the Olympics: 60-odd glaciers occupying a total area of less than 25 square miles, compared to more than 10 times that many glaciers in the Cascade Range. Thus if all the Olympic glaciers should melt away next season the regional result might be catastrophic but the global result would be negligible; neither sea level nor sea salinity would be appreciably affected. But all of the Olympic glaciers are constantly at work getting and spending huge quantities of moisture, resculpting the mountains, transporting rock downhill—and they are not about to melt away.

What keeps these alpine glaciers healthy are the moisture-laden winds that blow in from the ocean all year. More than 100 feet of snow may descend on them in the course of a winter, and the cool summer breezes retard melting. Because of these favorable conditions, the snowline—the level above which snow stays on the ground all year —is about 6,000 feet here, and in some years it creeps down to 4,000 feet on north-facing slopes. So there are large areas of the peaks where the snow always lies, keeping the glaciers well supplied. Blue Glacier carries the greatest burden of ice and has been the most intensively studied. Even though it lies 19 miles from the nearest road end, glaciologists have found its location and dimensions (2.6 miles long, about a mile wide, up to 900 feet thick) useful as a natural laboratory.

The scene this high on Olympus is not a forbidding one. In wintertime it does get stormy, with winds up to 100 miles per hour; but in the summer it is quite mild, a serene, pristine locale. Nor is it as lifeless a place as it appears to be. In the morning after we got there, two rosy finches flew past the huts; and later, while we were climbing back down the Snow Dome, a pair of daredevil ravens swooped in front of us. At evening the birds simply glide down to their nests in the warmer forests. Even on the barren surface of the glacier, there is something for the birds to eat: ice worms. These dark, inch-long annelids, kin of the earthworm, are members of a select community, the cryophilic, or cold-loving, permanent residents of this not-quite-frozen world. Their neighbors are a variegated lot, ranging from microscopic diatoms, protozoa and snow algae to snow fleas and daddy longlegs that get blown up by storms and somehow survive, at least for a while.

Ed LaChapelle rather likes the little ice worm, whose name—*Mesenchytraeus solifugus*—is longer than its body, and in his book, *Glacier*

Ice, he devotes a few friendly words to the species. "The ice worm probably has one of the most remarkable temperature environments of any creature on earth. His entire life cycle is spent very close to the freezing point of water." Apparently the ice worm retreats from the surface during the day to avoid the sun's heat, but it comes out in the evening or during cloudy weather, presumably to search for food. When a cold night starts to freeze the water at the surface, according to LaChapelle, the ice worm retreats down into the glacier once more, this time to get away from colder, subfreezing temperatures.

The algae that provide fodder for the ice worm are the same plants that create the phenomenon of "red snow" on the glacier, and they seem to follow the same up-and-down migration habits. *Chlamydomonas nivalis* is probably the most common of more than 100 varicolored species of snow algae. On Blue Glacier it appears in patches a few inches to several yards across, some blood red and some watermelon pink. To me it even smells and tastes a little like watermelon, but I've been told that it may have a laxative effect. Possessed of chlorophyll and able to utilize sunlight in photosynthesis, the single-celled alga is an incredibly prolific pasturage for the worms; the bright-red colonies have been estimated to contain half a million cells in a single milliliter, or .06 of a cubic inch.

No species of higher plant life can grow on the glacier itself, but an occasional clump of blossoms pokes out from the lateral moraine along its course. Among the flowers that appear up here in the Alpine zone (above 5,500 feet) are the eight endemics of the Olympic mountains, plants that are found nowhere else on earth; they have managed to survive the ice age on the high ridges above the level of ice that wiped out all vegetation at lower altitudes. The tenacious eight are the Olympic rattleweed, two varieties of Piper bellflower, the Flett violet, the Flett fleabane, the Olympic mountain butterweed, the mountain wallflower and the rock spirea. Nobody ever gets to see all eight in one visit because they bloom at different times and places during the brief summer season, but anyone lucky enough to see a single blossom, say the diminutive star-shaped blue jewel of the Piper bellflower, has to marvel at how hardy a perennial can be.

Like every glacier, the Blue began with a single snowflake that stuck —how many thousands of years ago no one knows. Also like every glacier, the Blue grew in size and strength because it consistently received more snowflakes in winter than it disbursed as meltwater in summer.

Cracked by the stresses of its descent, Blue Glacier spreads a broad blanket of ice beneath the 7,976-foot West Peak of Mount Olympus.

Some of the snow that lands in the cirques, or gathering basins, above the ice fall becomes part of the annual nonmelting accumulation, and may not leave the glacier for a century or more, until it is finally disgorged down at the glacier's snout. It does not remain in snow-crystal form, though; within days or, at most, a few weeks after snowflakes fall on the glacier their fragile, infinitely varied crystal structure disintegrates into tiny pellets called firn, much like the granular "corn snow" that skiers enjoy. At first fluffy and loose, the pellets become denser and more closely packed as the weight of later snows forces the air out of them. After some years they may be transformed into giant crystals of ice, which range from a fraction of an inch in diameter to a foot or more in length and which can occur by the millions in a glacier. The crystals still retain minute bubbles of air and eventually, by analysis of the oxygen and oxygen isotopes contained in the bubbles of very old ice crystals, glaciologists may be able to determine what the earth's atmosphere was like centuries ago.

Blue Glacier's own crystals and snows and its ebbs and flows have been observed since 1938 when Olympic National Park was established. The present research station was built during 1957-1958, the International Geophysical Year, and since then the Blue's anatomy and the state of its health have been under close scrutiny by teams from the University of Washington and California Institute of Technology. One subject of study has been the glacier's rate of flow, or rather its rates, for a glacier moves at different speeds in different places along its length. Down its ice fall, for instance, it moves fastest; it is slowed on its bottom as it slides and grinds over bedrock, and along its sides, where it plucks and quarries the rock. These varied movements set up the tremendous strains that result in crevasses. Blue Glacier's average movement forward is about five inches a day; since its tongue melts back at about the same rate, it is in a stable condition.

The Washington team led by LaChapelle has pursued a complex inquiry into the relationship between regional climate and the glacier's snow accumulation and evaporation and melting rates. Probing that relationship, in which a very small change in climate will have a noticeable effect on the glacier's growth, they have prowled its surfaces and its rocky moraines like Lilliputians swarming over Gulliver. At the time of our visit they were extracting cores of 100-year-old ice from deep within the glacier, using a windlass mounted on a steel tripod, for microscopic study of the crystal structures. At other times they have lowered cameras on cables all the way through the glacier to photograph ice in the act of scouring the bedrock below. In fact, in 1967 the Washington and Caltech scientists—for whom no herculean effort seems to be too much trouble—actually drove a six-foot tunnel almost 300 feet into the heart of the ice fall to the rock below, using chain saws and compressed-air jackhammers to chop their way through. (At the bottom of the tunnel, the men discovered that in places there are gaps between ice and rock big enough for a man to crawl through.) The mass of surrounding ice pressed one part of the tunnel walls back together in two weeks, but that was enough time for the researchers to study the various changes in the glacier's structure that occur as it flows slowly downgrade.

At the top of the glacier the firn is laid down in orderly layers, just as sedimentary rock is laid down on the ocean floor. In slowly spilling down the ice fall, the layers are destroyed and become as jumbled as the debris from an avalanche. Later, deformed by relentless pressure from ice on top and distorted by contact with bedrock, the ice is re-formed, in a process known as foliation, into different kinds of layers, no longer parallel to the ground, whose tops often form bands or striations on the glacier surface.

The Blue has also had its temperature taken as regularly as a hospital patient and has been found to be a "warm" glacier; that is, all its ice seems to be just at the freezing point, which is normal temperature for a glacier in a temperate environment. The ice in Antarctic and Greenland glaciers is 20° to 50° colder—and a cube of glacial ice from either Frigid Zone would last that much longer in a martini on the rocks.

LaChapelle's team has also found out that though Blue Glacier has not moved farther down the mountain in the past 15 years, it has nevertheless become a tiny but measurable amount bigger. Is this a sign of a slight cooling shift in climate, signaling the beginning of another ice age? No one is prepared to say on the evidence so far. But I'm betting that if Blue Glacier has any important secrets to reveal about the past or the future, Ed LaChapelle and his colleagues will find them.

A Vanguard of Mountaineers

For decades after Seattle was settled in 1852 its residents stared in wonderment at the mysterious Olympic Peninsula across Puget Sound. It was a monstrous provocation: largely unmapped, most of its peaks unclimbed. Not until 1890 was it traversed by a group of explorers, who took nearly six months to do it.

By the time of President Teddy Roosevelt, exponent of the strenuous life, the idea of *terra incognita* had become intolerable. The Olympic wilderness simply had to be taken on, and so on July 24, 1907, a group of local residents boarded a steamer and headed up the sound.

There were more than 70 men and women in the expedition—a band of those newfangled conservationists organized not long before into the Seattle Mountaineers Club. Among them were doctors, lawyers, teachers, librarians, plus four teenagers.

Arrangements for the three-week trek were precise: each person was to have one dunnage bag, weight limit 30 pounds; one pair of stout boots studded with cone-headed Hungarian or hob nails; reveille would be at 4:30; in camp, the women were to wear skirts over their bloomers, and bloomers without skirts on the trail.

The steamer deposited its passengers at Port Angeles and after a four-day walk they made base camp at Elwha Basin in the central Olympics. They fished virgin streams, posed for snapshots and glissaded down snowy slopes. It was not all fun —blizzards closed in, rain soaked blankets, climbers were hurt—but the setbacks only kindled an optimism peculiar to that innocent age. A doctor treated the injured, and difficulties were forgotten in convivial candy pulls around a campfire.

The pioneer jaunt also made history. On August 13, Mount Olympus' 7,976-foot West Peak, loftiest of the Olympics, was bested for the first time—by 11 dauntless Mountaineers, 10 men and a woman.

Six years later, club members returned to the peninsula, 106 strong, with the same good cheer, cartwheel hats and swaddling garb. In fact, of the photographs shown on the next pages, it is hard to distinguish those of one expedition from those of the other. The chief difference was that the 1913 Mountaineers, instead of returning the way they had come, went right on across the peninsula and emerged gaily on a Pacific beach, ready for one last blazing campfire.

Enthusiastic climbers of the Seattle Mountaineers' 1913 expedition, more than half of them women, perch triumphantly atop Mount Olympus' 7,780-foot East Peak. Members of the group's 1907 foray had scaled West Peak, the mountain's tallest.

Participants in the 1913 trip queue up on the Quinault River bank to await their turn while a woman hiker crosses the swift water on logs, steadying herself by a rope. In all, the party crossed and recrossed the North Fork of the Quinault five times. Later, in 28 dugout canoes poled by Indians, they swept through rapids to the Pacific.

Eleanor Chittenden, of the 1907 party, reflects an angler's pride as she shows her catch—one of the peninsula's teeming population of salmon.

Mollie Leckenby, like Eleanor a teenager on the 1907 expedition, snuggles down with her pet collie, Bob, apparently a freeloader on the trip.

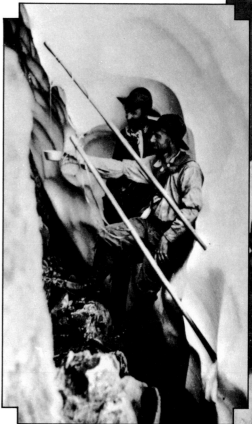

Their faces greased against the sun, Mountaineers of the 1913 party tackle the slopes of 6,246-foot Mount Seattle. Of the 84 people who began the assault, all but five made it to the top.

During an ascent of Mount Queets, two Mountaineers pause to catch a drink of meltwater, their alpenstocks thrust into a huge snowbank.

After a climb up Mount Noyes comes an exhilarating reward—sliding back down. The adventurers sprawled down every which way, arms and legs atangle. "Dangerous?" wrote one of them. "Possibly, but so funny!"

Members of the 1907 expedition raise Old Glory on a makeshift flagpole at their base camp in Elwha Basin in the heart of the Olympics. Here

hey lived for more than two weeks, and around nightly campfires told jokes, swapped favorite limericks and planned assaults on nearby peaks.

3/ Echoes of the Indian Past

*There was a time when our people covered the whole land
as the waves of a wind-ruffled sea cover its shell-paved floor.*

CHIEF SEATTLE/ *AT A POWWOW OF PUGET SOUND TRIBES, 1854*

The trail leads through more than three miles of glacier-bulldozed prairies and spruce forests before it comes out of the trees just below Cape Alava, where the Olympic Peninsula juts farthest into the Pacific. Ahead is another kind of forest—a prone forest of driftwood. Beyond it lie a strip of sand and a wide zone of rocks and tidal pools, and beyond that more rocks and three small pine-topped islands that break the incoming ocean waves. At low tide a large rusted anchor sticks out of the water, attached to festoons of heavy chain; it is about all that is left of the freighter *Austria,* wrecked here in a brutal winter storm in 1887. A three-foot-wide cleared path winds seaward through the jumble of rocks; long ago the Makah Indians who lived here pushed the boulders aside to make a dragway for their whaling canoes. Nearby are two sandstone pillars where a pair of bald eagles roost every morning. A little to the north of their perch rise the steep cliffs of Tskawahyah, also called Cannonball Island after the sandstone spheres that litter its base. These curious basketball-shaped lumps of rock, called concretions, were formed and cemented in the sandstone by waterborne minerals, and as the softer rock around them succumbed to wave action they tumbled from the cliffs.

On a nameless nearby rock, whitened by sea-bird droppings, a half-dozen Steller sea lions sometimes haul out to bask and bark. They are too far from shore and from the routes of fishing boats for anybody to bother them much. But on my last visit to Cape Alava, a young elephant seal—a larger relative of the Steller sea lion—swam past their rock and flopped onto the sands to die. He bore a tag that had been affixed by a California research station—and several gunshot wounds. There are commercial and sport fishermen who keep rifles handy on their boats to take pot shots at anything in the water that moves. Their rationalization for shooting the seals is that seals eat fish. So they do, but not enough to be shot for it.

Apart from that depressing episode I found Alava, as always, a pleasant place to be. Here, more than anywhere else along the Northwest coast, it is possible to glimpse the way of life this seaside wilderness imposed on its ancient inhabitants. For thousands of years the whale-hunting Makah Indians repeatedly chose the natural terrace above this beach as the site for a succession of villages, despite the slides of mud and clay that periodically buried them. One of the Makah art forms has survived the slides. Not far from the terrace is an aggregation of boulders inscribed with petroglyphs, crude but vivid rock carvings of human figures and little whales within pregnant whales. One drawing is provocatively cryptic, a depiction of a ship under sail looking a little like one of Christopher Columbus' own fleet. I ran my finger along its laboriously incised outline and wondered whose ship it might have been —Drake's *Golden Hind* or Cook's *Resolution* or some early Spanish caravel? Did it just sail past in vain search for gold and spices, or did it stop to send men ashore?

Here at Cape Alava an accident of nature has revealed a find unique in American archeology: the well-preserved remains of several Makah houses dating back at least 500 years. All of them were in one site, with living levels that may date back as far as 4,000 years; like the builders of the seven cities of Troy, the Makah erected one community on the ruins of another. From time to time the forested hillside above their terrace, loosened by storms, would give way all at once, inundating the latest settlement in a flood of clay. In the winter of 1970, long after the site had been abandoned, a section of the bank slumped away, exposing successive layers of houses and previous clay slides. When Dr. Richard Daugherty, head of the anthropology faculty at Washington State University, went to investigate, he found a mass of artifacts from a 500-year-old village—paddles, yew bows, fishing gear, baskets—sticking out of the bank. These objects had all been sealed in the clay of previous slides, unaffected by oxidation and bacterial action.

Daugherty, who had made some previous probes of the site, gathered a dedicated crew of students, faculty and young Makah from the tribe's present headquarters at Neah Bay 15 miles to the north. This group has been excavating the site ever since. They have carefully hosed thousands of objects from the clay, immersed them in a solution of polyethylene glycol that prevents them from rotting, and transported them to the archeological laboratory at Neah Bay for cataloguing and safekeeping. I lingered at the laboratory over two impressive items lovingly fashioned by skilled artisans among the pre-Columbian wilderness dwellers. One was a 12-foot house plank, a wide cedar slab with the silhouette of an open-mouthed whale carved on it. The other was a wooden replica of a whale's dorsal fin, painstakingly inlaid with 700 sea-otter teeth and obviously the prized display piece in the house of a Makah whale hunter. Looking at it and touching it, I longed for the impossible: to know and talk with its original owner.

To Dr. Daugherty, the site at Alava is as fascinating as Troy or Pompeii. "Archeologists generally have to deal with nonperishable items," he explained one day when we were poking around the dig. "I mean the potsherds and the stone things—the building blocks and so forth. The vegetable items, which probably form the bulk of any early culture, decay—just don't exist any longer. But here we do have these items. Along with the stones and bones we find blankets and hats and baskets, a regular cornucopia of things made from wood, bark and other plant fibers—the things the people used every day. Everything but animal tissue has survived intact.

"Scientifically it's all very important," Dr. Daugherty said, "but it's important for other reasons too. Just imagine a bunch of elderly Makah over at Neah Bay these days, telling their young people how great things were in the distant past, and the youngsters not paying much attention to such ramblings, or even believing. Suddenly they find it's all true and better than anyone thought. All the art works, the whaling and sealing implements we've recovered here have caused a real cultural revitalization in the tribe. Now they have a background, a rich heritage that nobody can deny."

Bountiful as the Makah corner of the world was in many ways, it was poor in metal ores. The people had to use their ingenuity to make stones, shells, animal bones and teeth do the work that in other contemporary societies was done by metal. Thus the unearthing at the Alava dig of a few iron tools dating from approximately the 15th Century—a 10-inch knife, a tiny exquisitely formed hatchet head used as a chisel—was puzzling. Had the metal fallen from the sky in meteorites?

Carvings of two killer whales, two moonlike faces and the head of an unidentifiable animal (at lower right) appear on sandstone slabs on the beach one mile south of Cape Alava. These cryptic petroglyphs are relics of the once-thriving culture of the whale-hunting Makah Indians, who occupied the nearby site for more than 2,000 years, abandoning it in the early 1900s.

Or had it been traded from tribe to tribe across the continent? More likely it came from across the Pacific in some Oriental vessel that stopped, or was wrecked, along this shore. Even a thousand years before Columbus the Chinese had ships that could go anywhere—with three and four decks and enormous crews. The first expedition from China to the eastern Pacific is believed to have been made in 458 A.D. by a Buddhist monk, Hwui Shan. Court records of the Liang Dynasty indicate that he evidently sailed across the ocean to Mexico, which he called the Wonderful Land of Fusang, after a plant to which he had given that name. (It may have been the century plant.)

For all anyone knows, no other ships appeared on the western horizon until 1579. In that year Sir Francis Drake, fresh from plundering Spanish settlements in California, merely glimpsed the wooded shores and headlands, cheekily called "all these Northerne coasts" New Albion, or New England, and hastened westward around the world in the *Golden Hind*. It was not until the 18th Century that the end began for the long era in which the Indians had the wilderness to themselves. The Russians swarmed over from Siberia, the Spanish edged north from California, the British and the Yankees came around Cape Horn—all in search of nonexistent continents and the Northwest Passage; and failing that, in ruthless quest for fortunes in furs.

The Russians were first, if not worst. For the greater glory and enrichment of Czar Peter the Great, their fur hunters, the *promyshleniki*, massacred sea lions and seals, sea otters and beavers, and any coastal Indians who got in their way. One casualty of their invasion was the sea cow, a gigantic animal that once flourished all along the Pacific coast but was already scarce when Vitus Bering's expedition encountered it in 1741. At 25 feet in length and 10 tons in weight, the toothless, vegetarian sea cow was nearly twice the size of its tropical relatives, the manatee and the dugong. Its hide was tough but its flesh was as flavorful as beef, and its thick layering of fat even tastier than that of other sea mammals. The sea cow was also clumsy, slow and an easy target. In less than three decades, the *promyshleniki* wiped the sea cow from the face of the earth.

The sea otters narrowly escaped the same fate. Their slaughter, begun by the Russians, was to go on—by arrow, by spear, by club and later by gun—until this century, when an international treaty put a stop to the carnage. From an estimated 150,000, the otter population had dwindled to near extinction; today it is back up to about 50,000, with a number of thriving colonies in residence off the Northwest coast.

Anyone lucky enough to have seen a sea otter in the wild is unlikely to forget it. This whiskered animal with the comical face and paddle tail is like no other on earth in appearance and behavior. Five feet long when fully grown, *Enhydra lutris* is the smallest sea mammal and the largest member of the family *Mustelidae,* which also includes the skunk and the weasel, the mink, the badger and the river otter. It is the choosiest of its kin in habitat, occupying a narrow ecological niche inside the 30-fathom depth line on the open seacoast. Within this area it likes to congregate in kelp beds in large groups called rafts, 100 otters or more to a raft. Why the otter favors this formation is not known; it is quite capable of thriving in parts of the open sea where there are no kelp beds at all. But the kelp, draped across the otter's body, does prevent it from drifting off from its fellow otters while it sleeps, and the kelp bed may also help smooth the turbulence of the waves.

The first thing you notice about the sea otter, unless it is hauled out on dry land, is that it spends most of its time flat on its back, whether awake or asleep, swimming or seeming to meditate. It is well able to swim belly-down and dive for food, but once it bobs up it floats on its back, placing a sea urchin or abalone on its stomach to be eaten at leisure. With a clam or mussel, it may also bring up a stone, which it will place on its stomach to smash the shell against. This tool-using behavior works well enough to help the otter consume a fifth of its body weight in food every day.

The otter spends a lot of time preening and grooming itself, and needs to. Unlike the whale or sea lion, it has no layer of blubber to keep it warm; instead, the inner hairs of its thick coat (an adult has up to a billion dark brown or ebony hairs) keep an insulating layer of air trapped against the skin. If the fur gets dirty, water may penetrate to the skin and the otter may become fatally chilled; it resorts to frequent grooming to prevent that, and even seems to squirm around inside its baggy skin to clean every inch of its fur with its forepaws. The otter's flexibility also enables it to curl up in a ball and turn graceful forward or backward somersaults in the water. But on land, which its ancestors forsook over a million years ago, it is utterly awkward, and when frightened goes galumphing back to water, looking for all the world like something hobbled for a potato-sack race.

But it is that rich, thick coat that made the sea otter responsible for the exploration—and exploitation—of the Northwest coast. One of the first men to sense the otter's potential value was the celebrated Captain

James Cook. When Cook put in at Nootka Sound, on the west coast of Vancouver Island, on his last voyage of exploration in 1788, he took aboard his *Resolution* a number of sea-otter pelts. Cook was killed in the Hawaiian Islands, but when his crew sailed on to China they found that people were eager to pay fabulous prices for the furs. Cook had written in his journal, "the fur of these animals . . . is certainly softer and finer than that of any others we know of, and therefore, the discovery of this part of the continent of North America, where so valuable an article of commerce may be met with, cannot be a matter of indifference." Thomas Paine later called these animals "Nootka catskins," and still later Lewis and Clark referred to them as "sea-orter polecats." Lewis noted in his journal: "it is the richest and I think the most delicious fur in the world at least I cannot form an idea of any more so. It is deep thick silkey in the extreme and strong."

Long before Lewis and Clark, word went around the world that the Russians and Captain Cook's men had gotten on to something good. Dozens of fur companies were competing in the hunt for sea-otter skins. The Indians, who had always taken the sea otter for granted—its flesh was not especially good to eat—soon realized they were fools to sell for a few fishhooks or nails a fur that would bring hundreds of dollars on some faraway market. But when they began to sell the pelts more dearly, battles with the traders ensued.

The savagery of the combat may be illustrated by one notable encounter that the Indians won decisively. Their foes were recent intruders in the wilderness; the Indians were an immemorial and integral part of it, as well adapted to it as were the great cedars from which they shaped their whaling canoes and totem poles. The wilderness was their mentor as well as their home, and one of the things it taught them about survival was the value of surprise attack. They had seen how the eagle swoops down on the unsuspecting salmon, how the cougar leaps out of a tree onto the back of a passing elk, how the killer whale rushes from behind to engulf the seal in sudden death. The Indians put such lessons to use. When a European ship sent a boat ashore to fill water casks, the Indians, like as not, would descend on the oarsmen without warning, butcher them, and smash the boat to extract the nails and fittings. When one tribe attacked another, stealth and surprise were as important as strength: a moonless night, blackened skins and silent paddles were what ensured victory. Only at the last minute would the blood-curdling war whoops sound.

So it was natural for Maquina, chief of the Nootka—the parent tribe of the Makah—to count on surprise as he plotted revenge on the whites who had appeared in his Vancouver Island domain sometime in the spring of 1803. In a quarter century of dealing with fur traders and explorers of various nationalities, Maquina had accumulated plenty of grievances. At the moment he was angry about a double-barreled fowling piece that John Salter, captain of the ship *Boston,* had given him. The lock was broken; he thought it a shoddy weapon to give a chief. And when he sought to return it, the gun was rudely seized and tossed to the ship's armorer for repair.

Insulted, and aiming to divide by cunning and conquer by surprise, Maquina devised a ruse. He and his braves boarded the *Boston* for a friendly visit and informed Salter that a run of salmon had appeared in a nearby river. The captain sent 10 of his sailors off on a fishing trip. For a time the Indians carried on the pretense of amiability; then, on Maquina's signal, they drew their knives. Below deck at work, young John Jewitt, the armorer, heard the uproar and rushed up a companionway, only to tumble back when an Indian took a swipe at him with an ax, gashing him in the head. Maquina—who knew by then how skillfully Jewitt could forge iron fishhooks—decided to spare the youth, and locked him in a cabin below decks to prevent the braves from dispatching him. When Jewitt was finally brought topside, he saw 25 of his shipmates' heads, including those of the members of the fishing

JEWETT PLEADING FOR THOMPSON.   THE SHIP BOSTON IN FLAMES.   MAQUINA'S RETURN FROM WHALING.

party, arrayed in a grisly row. The only other crew member not killed was a sailmaker named Thompson, who was spared when Jewitt convincingly pleaded that the man was his father. The *Boston* itself did not survive. An Indian prowling the hold for loot set the ship afire with his torch, and the biggest vessel yet to visit Nootka Sound blew up, leaving Jewitt and Thompson stranded on a hostile shore near an inlet called, of all things, Friendly Cove.

For nearly three years they lived among the Nootka as slaves, not mistreated but not allowed to leave. Jewitt made himself useful by fashioning tools and weapons out of metal salvaged from the ship, and by serving as a companion to Maquina's son. The chance to escape came in 1805 when the brig *Lydia,* also out of Boston, put in at Friendly Cove to inquire what had happened to the *Boston.* Regally daubed with ocher, Maquina went aboard, carrying a note from Jewitt—an appeal for rescue that the captive had carefully mistranslated for his captor as a message of welcome. The *Lydia's* skipper read it and forthwith clapped the chief in irons. A speedy exchange of prisoners followed, during which Maquina hinted that he rather admired Jewitt's own capacity for contriving surprises, and declared that he would miss him greatly. Jewitt was later to produce a bestseller about his captivity (below), a book that for years few sailors were without on their voyages around the globe.

The rescue ship *Lydia* sailed south, and in November stopped at the

TAKING THE BEAR.   PARTING OF JEWETT AND MAQUINA.

Illustrations from John Jewitt's early-19th Century account of his life as a captive of Maquina, a wily Indian chief of the Northwest coast, depict five episodes of his experience. Left to right: a kneeling Jewitt (his name is misspelled in the old captions) begs for his shipmate's life; the pair bemoan their ship's burning; Maquina's braves hail his dispatch of a whale with a harpoon made by Jewitt; a bear steps into a trap—a salmon-baited plank, which, when yanked, looses a load of stones; finally, the captives go free.

mouth of the Columbia River. But the captain missed a chance to give a ride back East to some other Americans far from home. The local Indians never told him that Meriwether Lewis and William Clark were encamped nearby, though they showed him medals that had been given them as souvenirs. Nor did the Indians tell Lewis and Clark that a ship was anchored a few miles from where they were building their makeshift Fort Clatsop in which, desperately short of supplies, they would spend the soggy, dismal winter.

So the *Lydia* sailed on, and it would take another year for Lewis and Clark to complete their grueling return trip back over the mountains and across the plains to St. Louis to complete the epic transcontinental journey of discovery on which President Thomas Jefferson had sent them. Their hardships in the far western wilderness exceeded any John Jewitt endured at Nootka. "Ocian in view! O! the Joy," Clark had written in his notebook when they first approached salt water. But within a few days, after they tried camping on the north bank of the Columbia, where great combers from the Pacific crashed on the unsheltered shore, Clark's journal entries were joyless:

"At 2 o'clock the flood tide came in accompanied by immense waves and heavy winds, floated the trees . . . and tossed them about. . . . Every exertion and the strictest attention by every individual of the party was scarcely sufficient to save our canoes from being crushed by these monstrous trees, many of them nearly two hundred feet long and from four to seven feet through. . . . The logs on which we lie are all afloat every high tide. The rain continues all day. We are all wet, also our bedding and many other articles. . . . Nothing to eat but pounded fish." Still, Lewis and Clark and their party withstood the rigors of the coast. Behind them they left their miserable fort and a memorial carved in the bark of a nearby tree: "William Clark December 3rd 1805. By land from the U. States in 1804 & 1805."

At that time the wilderness still belonged to the Indians, though the course of empire already had been set. In another half century or so the tribes would be overrun, their complex culture impoverished, their gene pools irrevocably altered, their blood streams infected by civilized man's diseases. In a way the wilderness itself was their undoing: it was so rich in furs and fish and timber that sooner or later the outside world was bound to discover it and move in, thrust the Indians aside and take over.

Yet the Indians staved off the inevitable for an uncommonly long

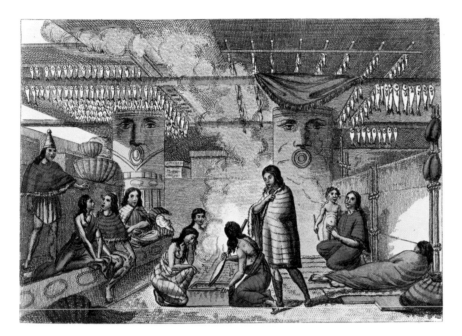

A Nootka lodge served as both communal home and fishery. Salmon, halibut and cod for storage were hung from racks to dry and were smoked over alder fires. Fish and blubber for immediate eating were boiled or steamed in tubs of water fueled by hot stones. Huge heads carved and painted on posts (rear) added to the décor. The Nootka wore capes and conical hats made of the inner part of cedar bark woven with dog's hair and goat's wool.

time while enjoying an uncommonly abundant way of life. In most years their subsistence came easily from the wild land and sea. There were hordes of salmon and halibut to trap and hook, sea lions and seals to spear, game animals galore to kill with bow and arrow, shellfish for the digging, berries for the picking, birds to catch in nets strung between tall poles. Herring eggs, which the Indians considered a great delicacy, were obtainable in winter and spring simply by immersing a hemlock bough in salt water; the spawned eggs soon attached in clusters to the branches and needles. Strands of kelp provided strong, pliant fishlines; strips of cedar bark made rain hats and cloaks as well as intricately woven baskets.

With all this natural bounty, the Indians had little need for agriculture —apparently tobacco is about the only plant they cultivated—and they had both the wealth and time for life's amenities. The most notable of these was a feast they called the potlatch, a ritual to which a chief would invite friends and rivals for the purpose of emphasizing his status and his wealth—which he would then distribute to his guests. According to rank they received food and clothing, weapons and art objects, even slaves, and as a final show of his disregard for material things the host might even burn the potlatch house down. On such occasions it was more productive, as well as more blessed, to give than to receive, for each guest of high rank was expected to return the favor, and then some, at a potlatch of his own.

The coastal Indians ranged from squat and ugly to tall and comely. They bathed as often as twice a day—more than most white men and women of the 18th Century—but their houses and their garments reeked of rancid fish oil and whale blubber; in times of food shortages they would throw a sea-otter pelt over a steaming pot, to flush out and eat the vermin infesting the fur. Yet certain strong and highly admirable values were held by the Nootka of Vancouver Island and their cousins to the south, the Makah. These were the people of the whale, who paddled far out into the Pacific in eight-man crews to capture the great gray monsters of the deep. Their courage, their singleness of purpose, their passion for their calling were as keen as Captain Ahab's, and so was their constant awareness that any whale-hunting expedition might be their last.

The head man of the crew was the harpooner, who also had to be a chief or someone of high tribal standing and wealth. Whenever he headed out to sea, his wife would come down to the shore, staring after the canoe; then she would go into seclusion in her house, not to come out, or eat or drink, until her husband's return. It was believed that such quietude would magically influence the behavior of the whales. At sea, meanwhile, the men would stalk their prey. When the high-prowed canoe, some 45 feet long, hewn from cedar and steamed to a beam of seven feet, came near a whale, the paddlers would maneuver alongside, carefully steering clear of the flukes. The harpooner would drive his lance into the animal near the head; floats made of sealskin were attached to the line. Many such floats, as the battle went on, would make it harder and harder for the whale to sound.

When the harpooner had plunged his bone-barbed weapon home, legend claims that he would sing out this lengthy incantation, beseeching the victim's cooperation:

"Whale, I have given you what you are wishing to get—my good harpoon. And now you have it. Please hold it with your strong hands and do not let go. Whale, turn toward the beach and you will be proud to see the young men come down to see you; and the young men will say to one another: 'What a great whale he is! What a fat whale he is! What a strong whale he is!' And you, whale, will be proud of all that you will hear them say of your greatness. Whale, do not turn outward but hug the shore, and tow me to the beach of my village, for when you come ashore there, the young men will cover your great body with bluebill duck feathers and with the down of the great eagle, the chief of all birds; for this is what you are wishing, and this is what you are trying to find from one end of the world to the other, every day you are traveling and spouting."

If the hunters were lucky, and the harpoon well placed, the whale may have obliged them by succumbing without much of a fight. More often, probably, the whalers were in for a long, perilous running fight in which seamanship and simple courage counted for more than incantations. No doubt many a whaler's wife never saw her man again. But the Indians were skilled in their art, and one way or another the whale usually ended up on the beach.

There the villagers made good on the harpooner's flowery promises —and then the whale was butchered. The saddle under the dorsal fin was the harpooner's by right, a keepsake symbolic of his prowess. Huge chunks of blubber and meat were divided among the crew and the rest of the villagers, the blubber to be cooked down for oil. Within a day, the monumental carcass would be stripped down to the bone and left for the tides and the scavenging animals to take away.

Little exists today at Nootka Sound to testify to such great enterprises of the past; the people are gone, their tall totem poles have been carted away and their houses have rotted to nothingness, along with the canoes in which they entombed their dead in the branches of trees. It is only at the Cape Alava dig that the whaling Indians' way of wilderness life has come to light again, just as if it had been preserved in a set of time capsules.

NATURE WALK / In the Enchanted Valley

PHOTOGRAPHS BY DAVID CAVAGNARO

Spring takes its own good time coming to the Enchanted Valley, deep in the southwest corner of the Olympic Range. This secluded and aptly named enclave still sleeps under its blanket of snow in a high-sided crib of mountain walls long after the season's lengthening days have begun to awaken life only 13 miles downstream in the moist forests of the Quinault River. Even when spring does come it does not suffuse the valley all at once; it creeps from lower elevations to higher. Thus the lofty north-facing slopes are barely beginning to shrug off winter's embrace at a time when the bottomland is already ablaze with new growth.

To walk the length of the valley floor, 1,932 feet above sea level, and then up to chilly White Creek Basin, 2,000 feet higher, is to reverse the calendar, to climb backward in springtime. It is a little unsettling up there in the basin in the shirt-sleeve warmth of the noon sun; you almost want to tell the dormant flowers and shrubs to get a move on—don't they know spring has sprung? But then after a while, the sun starts to sink, the temperature drops, and you realize that spring is still really only a promise up here. The tardy flowers and shrubs know best.

It was the second week in June when we set out for the Enchanted Valley: Bill Lester, an Olympic National Park ranger who knows the peninsula as well as anyone, David Cavagnaro, with his cameras on his back, and I. The trail from Graves Creek Ranger Station snaked up along the Quinault, which rippled sedately in some places, dashed loudly by in others. It was a longish hike, and the daylight was mostly gone when we crossed the river on a foot log and sensed as much as saw that the thick forest had given way to the broad open mouth of the valley. We unpacked outside the old log chalet that serves hikers as a shelter, and soon realized that we were sharing its backyard with a yearling black bear. When he saw us he bear-hugged the trunk of a cottonwood, shinnied up it and sat among the branches for an hour, staring silently at us, before descending and ambling away in the darkness.

Morning light brought a clear view of our valley: a floor of grassland, dotted with black-cottonwood trees and red-alder thickets that screened the river; on the right a steep, wooded mountainside and on the left a great façade of rock. The cliff's upper pinnacles, a mile above, were

wreathed with clouds, but all along its face, seeming to pour right out of the sky, was a lacework of waterfalls. Some clung to the rocks; others leaped recklessly through hundreds of feet of space. Exploring, I crossed the river and hiked to the base of the cliff, where a vast snow avalanche had rumbled to a halt, prob-

INSIDE THE SNOW CAVE

ably only a few weeks earlier. The snow had been melted by water running under it, and the tunnel thus carved had been enlarged by the flow of warm air. The result was a snow cave with a double arcade at its entrance. I ducked inside to find the glistening walls of the cave scalloped into an arresting pattern and streaked with dirt from the mountainside. The cave's interior was greenish white, and echoed with the splash and drip of a small stream

THE ENCHANTED VALLEY, WALLED IN BY CLIFFS AND CLOUDS

that would soon join the river.

The great cliff that rose sharply behind the snow cave exposed its flank to the morning sun; the clear light revealed that this towering mass of sedimentary stone was a gigantic rock garden standing on end. I clambered up a few hundred feet for a closer look and realized that all about me spring was in full cry. Staring me in the face was a bouquet of Sitka columbine, straining outward to catch the sunlight, some of the bright blossoms framing a glimpse of distant Mount Anderson. The five-spurred petals of this flower look a little like the talons of an eagle—*aquila* in Latin, hence the columbine's generic name, *Aquilegia*.

I saw that I was not alone on the cliff. A quarter mile away a black bear, bigger than last night's visitor, was loping up the slope of another avalanche. (I am always amazed, and amused, by a bear's utter unconcern with the difference between uphill and downhill. It scoots up as fast as it runs down, or maybe faster.) This bear got to the top of the snowbank, then promptly trotted down again and disappeared in the thickets that bordered the river.

A few yards beyond the Sitka columbine, edging sideways and grabbing alder and huckleberry branches for support, I came upon a lovely two-foot-high Nootka rose bush. The blossoms were early; the plant seldom flowers at these altitudes before July. On some, the morning dew was still evaporating from the delicate pink petals. Nootka rose hips, the plant's seed pods, are rich in vita-

SITKA COLUMBINE IN THE CLIFF GARDEN

NOOTKA ROSE

HAIRY PAINTBRUSH AND AMERICAN HAREBELLS

min C, but reputed to be quite bitter. I have not eaten them, but have been told that freezing and thawing removes the bitterness and renders them quite tasty.

Nearby, brilliant tongues of flame caught my eye. They were blossoms of hairy paintbrush, alias northwestern paintbrush. The genus covers a wide spectrum of color, from light yellow through orange and scarlet to magenta, but this species ordinarily blooms fiery red. Here they were complemented by the delicate counterpoint of a scatter of blue American harebell flowers—also known as bluebells of Scotland.

The hairy paintbrush, like the columbine, attracts not bees—they are blind to bright red—but hummingbirds. Among the many other flowers that bees do go for is the paler, prickly bloom of the Indian thistle, which I encountered a little downslope from the paintbrush. Butterflies, too, find this native American thistle an addicting delicacy. It is also called edible thistle; the young stalks are quite tasty when peeled and boiled. The thistle's plump, succulent roots, too, are edible. They were baked in kilns by the Indians, a method Meriwether Lewis described in 1806 as giving the roots a flavor "exactly that of sugar." The thistle, he added, "is the sweetest vegetable employed by the Indians."

The morning was warming up, which meant I had to climb down from the cliff garden—where I could have spent the whole day happily —so that we could get a move on toward our goal, high on the opposite

INDIAN THISTLE

SUBALPINE SPIREA

OLYMPIC ONION

side of the valley. But I was fascinated by the flowers, which were strewn everywhere, more species than I knew or could even count; and I couldn't help lingering over a couple more. One was a rust-pink spray of the subalpine spirea. It is well named *Spirea densiflora*, "thick with flowers," for the blossoms contain innumerable long stamen filaments, each with a tiny pollen-laden anther at the tip, waiting for the next cooperative pollen gatherer—bee, butterfly or hummingbird—to pass by.

I also tarried over an Olympic onion, a member of the lily family, blooming amidst a fanfare of yellow violets. Its fleshy leaves, rising from the base of the stalk, formed graceful curls at their tips, like curlicues formed on strips of ribbon with a knife edge. Later the leaves would wither, but the bulb of the plant would remain edible. But for now, onions joined Nootka rose hips on my list of the Enchanted Valley's untried delicacies.

I picked my way down a rockslide, squished across the marshy thicket, recrossed the Quinault and rejoined the others to head up the Enchanted Valley toward the woods.

The grassy, pasture-like part of Enchanted Valley is only a few acres in extent. Walking up the valley you leave this flatland in a few minutes; the river and the trail more or less follow it, then pass in and out of clumps of conifers and spacious clearings; the latter showed signs of trampling and rolling by elk. Indeed, looking across the river at one point to where the cliff tapered down to

CRYSTAL PEAK FRAMED BY HEMLOCKS

meadow and woods, I glimpsed a herd of about 30 elk browsing lazily on a hillside, cinnamon colored against the green. A more permanent prospect, dazzlingly bright through the dark mountain hemlocks that dominate the forest at this level, was the wrinkled, craggy face of Crystal Peak, still far above us, since the trail had not yet begun to gain elevation appreciably. Yet we were obviously higher now—and earlier in springtime—than in our approach to the valley. Down there I had picked and eaten near-ripe salmonberries along the trail; up here they and the thimbleberries had just opened their blossoms.

A variety of ground covers carpeted the forest floor on both sides of the trail: three-leaved oxalis, looking like overblown clover; bunchberry, or Canadian dogwood, showing four creamy-white bracts, and around some lichen-covered rocks, a spread of deerfoot vanillaleaf, with timid little white blossoms poking up from green, maple-like leaves. The vanillaleaf, like many wild plants, has more than one name. It is charmingly called sweet-after-death because its leaves, when dried, have the smell of vanilla. They are also supposed to repel flies if hung in a room. Maybe, but in any case, they make the room smell good.

All these ground-cover plants are shade tolerant and indeed require subdued light; I have never seen them in clearings that get hours of direct sunlight every day. The same goes for a yellow slime mold, which thrives in well-shaded spots where

DEERFOOT VANILLALEAF

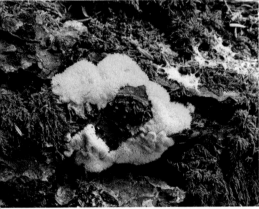

A YELLOW SLIME MOLD

A RED ADMIRAL, POISED

the light filters through thousands of conifer needles, but which would dry out and become dormant in a day or so if deprived of shade.

Except for the occasional zing of a bee or mosquito, and the steady rumble of the river from beyond the fringe of trees, the forest was quiet at midday: no sigh of wind, no call of bird, no roar of bear. A few butterflies flitted about, all nervous motion and no noise. One, a red admiral, came to rest on a branch as we approached, sat poised a few moments, then made a hasty take-off, disturbed either by our passing or by some signal we could not detect.

We stopped for lunch under an ancient hemlock. It was not just any hemlock: a battered old sign claimed it to be the world's largest recorded western hemlock, 8 feet 7 inches in diameter at breast height, circumference 27 feet 2 inches, and originally 200 feet tall—amended to 125 feet after a lightning bolt had snapped off the top. (The reason the sign was so battered is that an irritated bear had knocked it off its posts and chewed on it.) The tree is one of several unique giants in the Olympic forests, among them the world's largest western red cedar, the world's largest Douglas fir and the world's largest Sitka spruce. All owe their immensity to mild climate, abundant rainfall and accidents of location with respect to other trees, drainage, soil and positioning on a slope.

This hemlock, at least five centuries old and moss covered on the north side, nevertheless still had live branches low enough for me to reach

up and touch; it stood in a mound of its own half-inch needles and discarded cones, none more than an inch long. It had lost its drooping leader, or growing tip, along with the 75 feet of height that the lightning bolt had subtracted, but it was still majestic and vigorous, with the bright green of new growth flaunting

THE ANCIENT WESTERN HEMLOCK

bravely at the ends of its branches.

Here at the hemlock, the trail begins to climb the side of the valley, en route to Anderson Pass and O'Neil Pass. Also, not far from here is where the Quinault River comes tearing down out of the mountains and slows for its trip through Enchanted Valley proper. I wandered through a hemlock stand, crunching the diminutive cones underfoot, and came to the stream's edge.

Up here near its headwaters the east fork of the Quinault is small, fast and full of white water. It hurries downhill through an obstacle course of its own making—a field of boulders it has transported during freshets from glacial leftovers lying in the ravines upstream. Here and there the carcasses of great

A WOLF SPIDER

trees bridge the river, and rockslides have changed its path many times —though not enough to undermine the giant hemlock 100 yards away. Alongside the river's present bed is an expanse of rock and sand where it used to flow and where it still spills over at times of high water.

At first glance this abandoned bed looks inhospitable to life, a small wasteland of bare, tumbled stones and pulverized rock baking in the hot June sun. But only at first glance. After I had sat on a big warm boulder a few moments I realized that this alluvial flat in its stranded, arid way was as busy a rock garden as the big, verdant cliff I had climbed earlier in the day. Here there were

THE ROCKY QUINAULT, EMERGING FROM THE MOUNTAINS

Lilliputian hemlock, fir and cedar seedlings growing in close company among the rocks. These infant trees, sprung from bird-dropped or wind-blown seed, might not survive for very long but they were trying.

A large wolf spider stilted across a boulder—an unusual sight, because these hunters usually prowl at night, when the wasps that prey on them are asleep. There is no use looking for a wolf spider's web because it builds none, living instead in a hole or crevice from which it crawls to seek out, with eight sharp eyes, the insects on which it feeds.

A few yards away a brown garter snake sidled between two rocks, looking for shade. I walked over and gave it some—the shadow of my body—and it became still. Surprising myself with an unwonted quickness of hand, I picked up the snake and it flicked its tongue and squirmed violently; we looked each other in the eye for a moment and I released it to go on its way. It darted through a varicolored clump of budding stonecrop that crowded every inch of growing space in a jumble of rocks, then twisted past a bevy of tiny Star-of-Bethlehem flowers that surrounded a big rock tinted brown with iron oxide. When the snake had disappeared, I turned my back on the riverbed—again with reluctance—and walked back to the giant hemlock, where the trail begins its ascent of the valley wall.

Not long after we began our own ascent I became aware of a subtle, gradual change in vegetation: the western hemlocks were thinning out

A BROWN GARTER SNAKE

A CLUMP OF STONECROP

STAR-OF-BETHLEHEM

AVALANCHE CHUTES, SWEPT CLEAR OF TREES

and becoming intermixed with their smaller cousins, the mountain hemlocks, along with a few subalpine firs and slender alders.

I became much more forcefully aware of something else. On all sides I saw evidence of the violence that threatens life at every moment on these steeply pitched slopes. I mean the violence wrought by snow avalanches and rockslides. We had to make several precarious crossings of freshly tumbled snowbanks that loomed hundreds of feet above us and stretched hundreds of feet below. The trail was also frequently interrupted by rockslides, and we stepped with utmost care so as not to start new slides that could take us down with them. A trail crew had been up here to saw apart the bigger trees that had been flung across the trail during the winter's assaults, but more clearing remained to be done before the trail could be considered open for summer travel.

Snow still lay in some of the chutes cleared of trees by the avalanche's rampage. On many still-wet slopes alders trying to grow in the debris-filled path of avalanches lay almost prostrate but alive, exhibiting their particular capacity for survival: the trees had simply bent to let the masses of snow pass over them, and now were struggling to get erect again.

Amid all the evidence of violent attacks on it, the mountain's vegetation was stubbornly reasserting itself, but it was clear that spring was not nearly as far along up here as it was down below. The falsehellebore, which we had seen in tall, greenish-yellow bloom a thousand feet below us, was poking up its opulent leaves of vivid green but was still weeks away from blooming. Avalanche lilies, not many, were blossoming where snow had just melted off the ground. Later in the summer they would blanket the avalanche chutes in coverlets of white and yellow, then turn lavender at their season's end. But now only a few pioneers had appeared, living dangerously under the still-potent threat of more destruction from above.

Nearby, a bed of dark moss was punctuated with the insouciant red heads of matchstick lichen. Spreading over one shaded log were defiant knobs of orange yellow, the gelatinous fungus called witches'-butter.

YOUNG FALSEHELLEBORE

There were even a few young mountain huckleberries, translucent as salmon eggs, getting a late start in life on bushes that somehow had escaped the lethal snow slides.

In midafternoon we hopped across stones in a rushing creek that drains White Glacier, and reached a fork in the trail. We had come a bit more than three miles—and a world away —from the Enchanted Valley chalet. The left fork goes northeast to Anderson Pass; we took the right fork, which led to our destination, White Creek Basin. The trail became steeper, the snow patches more frequent and deeper. The tumbling Quinault was long since out of sight and out of earshot, far below.

After we had climbed a little, the trail simply got lost in the snow. By

PIONEERING AVALANCHE LILIES

MOUNTAIN HUCKLEBERRIES

now it was well into the afternoon and the stuff was mushy; we crashed upward, grabbing branches, stumbling, falling, getting our boots full of snow. Then we were on top and the snow was a little more solid, the terrain suddenly open. On one side of us was a tilted marsh, murmuring with meltwater and sprinkled with tiny elkslip marigolds, just beginning their brief flowering. The plants, also

we had climbed, and were rewarded with a more pleasing aspect. At our feet a scattering of subalpine buttercups were coming into bloom. Beyond the snow-patched basin, across the valley, the bulky mass of West Peak loomed directly in front of us. To its right was a sharp-peaked shoulder of Mount Anderson, the only mountain in the Olympics that drains into the Pacific on the west,

ELKSLIP MARIGOLD

called marsh marigolds, had the wet habitat they love, bathed in a crystalline flow of snowmelt.

On the other side of the basin White Creek poured down a little canyon. The source of the meltwater and of White Creek stood implacably before us: a tremendous white wall rising to the broken peak of Mount LaCrosse and to a high notch that is O'Neil Pass.

We turned around to see whence

the Strait of Juan de Fuca on the north and Hood Canal on the east. Between the peaks lay a glacier that is locally known as Hanging Glacier.

Now the clouds began to close in, while in the cold air two wrens called to each other. We headed downhill, scuffing through the snow that was getting crusty as the sun left it. We, too, were chilled as we began the descent, for here at 3,900 feet, spring was only beginning.

LOOKING ACROSS WHITE CREEK BASIN

4/ An Evergreen Kingdom

*The Olympic forests are what you imagined virgin forests
were when you were a child. They are tall as trees of fairy tale,
and dense as that.* DONALD CULROSS PEATTIE/ *THE NATURE OF THINGS*

The name of the horse was Nick and as far as he was concerned the
name of the game was caution. I spent three days with the big charcoal-
gray stallion and found him as trustworthy as they come, picking a
calm and careful way through all the tight spots of a hilly forest trail
that in places was only about 12 inches wide, hundreds of feet above a
fast-flowing river. Our one brush with disaster was not Nick's fault or
mine, but the fault of the trail itself.

We started out—four people, four horses and a mule—from Sol Duc
Hot Springs, a small spa in the north-central part of the Olympic Peninsula, on a route that was to cut southeastward, go up the north flank
of a divide, descend 4,000 feet through the woods on the west side, tra-
verse the valley of the Bogachiel rain forest and come out a few miles
from the old logging town of Forks. Roger Allin was in the lead of our
party; he had organized the trip because he was only in his first year as
superintendent of Olympic National Park and he had not yet toured the
Bogachiel, the wildest of the four rain forests found in his domain. Behind Roger rode my daughter Julie; I followed, with Dave Reaume, the
park's trail-system supervisor, bringing up the rear and towing the mule
that carried our gear.

The ascent was steep, and as we gained altitude the trees lost di-
mension. Towering four-foot-thick Douglas firs, sheathed in deeply
corrugated bark, rose all around us at first. For an hour we could reach

out and pick plump huckleberries from bushes that grew saddle-high along the trail. But as we zigzagged upward the bushes dwindled and the big trees gave way to thin spires of Alaska cedar and subalpine fir. The shaded higher slopes were chilly and pocketed with midsummer snowbanks. Then quite suddenly we came to the crest. A bronze marker set in the ground noted the elevation: 4,304 feet. We squinted into the bright sun; it was like coming out of a darkened theater into the brilliance of midday.

Ahead of us a grassy bank was ablaze with Indian paintbrush, blooming in little tongues of flame among cheerful blue blossoms of lupine. On this ridge long exposed to the elements the trees were sparse and small, some of them twisted by wind and snow into the bizarre shapes that the Germans call *krummholz*—literally, crooked wood. Beyond the dwarf trees, to the south, rose Bogachiel Peak and the multiple summits of Mount Olympus. To the southwest lay ridge after ridge of dark green hills, a rumpled carpet of trees.

What we were seeing was the biggest remnant of a western wildwood that had once stretched 3,000 miles along the Pacific coast. In its prime—thousands of years ago—this forest primeval held one of the world's largest collections of conifers, an evergreen belt mantling all the coastal ranges from Alaska deep into California, and piling up inland against the Cascades and the Sierra. It was a league of forest communities, dominated in the rainy north by giant firs, hemlocks, cedars and spruces and in the foggy south by even more gigantic redwoods, the tallest trees on earth.

We lunched there at the summit of the divide, enjoying a bird's-eye view that vanished almost as soon as we started down. Once more the trees closed in around us. Something about the firs and cedars struck me as curious; the lower parts of their trunks spread out horizontally a foot or so before shooting up. "That's because of the weight of the snow," Roger Allin explained. "It bent them downhill when they were young." After a while we caught a first glimpse of the Bogachiel River far below, running along in our direction but outpacing us. As we descended toward the river, the trail was again bordered with huckleberries, and where the ground was not covered with the outsized cloverleaves of oxalis it was strewn with what looked rather like Christmas corsages—clumps of bunchberry dogwood, with scarlet berries set in rosettes of bright green leaves.

From time to time we crossed small streams tumbling downhill to join the river. At each crossing the trail dropped sharply for a few yards, cut across the stream bed, then made a climbing turn up the far bank. It was at one such crossing that Nick and I almost came to grief. Just ahead, Roger and Julie had stopped in a shaft of sunlight. Roger said, "There's a picture," and pointed to the right. A spider had strung a 10-foot line between two spruces, woven a web the size of a steering wheel and now rested in the center of its handiwork. I reached into the saddlebag for my camera and backed Nick up a step in order to get a stronger backlight on the web. It was a serious misstep. The edge of the trail crumbled under Nick's hoof and he went down, rear feet clawing at the stream bank.

"Better get out of the stirrups," said Dave Reaume, behind me in midstream. I did, and flung myself off the saddle to get out of the way lest Nick fall on me. I came down hard on my back, on brush and rocks. Nick came tumbling after, but he got to his feet in the stream bed. "You all right?" Dave asked. I said, "I think so," but waited for him to get Nick back onto the trail before pulling myself up.

"Truth is, we don't maintain this trail much any more," Dave said, making me feel a little better.

"Where do you hurt?" Roger asked.

"Right back here," I said, rubbing the right rear bottom of my rib cage, which was already beginning to ache.

"I'm sorry, but you'll hurt worse tomorrow."

Julie said consolingly, "That was a nice cartwheel you turned. You sort of *flew* off the horse."

As we went on, I noticed an old trail sign carved on a board, identifying as Sunday Creek the spot where (it later turned out in X-rays) I had broken three ribs. It could have been worse. At the previous creek Nick and I would have fallen a lot farther.

Six times that day, as we rode lower into the forest, we disturbed swarms of yellow jackets. Each time our horses bolted, but nobody was thrown. Three times we saw black-tailed deer, which looked at us and went back to leaf-nibbling. Once a hefty, glossy black bear (they never undergo the brown or cinnamon phase here, for genetic reasons unknown) loped across our trail and crashed on through the brush, never looking at us. Twice, as we entered clearings, the buff-colored rumps of Roosevelt elk melted into the woods on the far side; the grass was beaten down where they had been browsing. Along the way we also overtook one fat garter snake. But except for three slim college-girl backpackers, we saw no other human being all day.

In a fern-carpeted Olympic forest a big-leaf maple (center) and a Sitka spruce benefit from the sunlight flooding into a tranquil glade.

There is no sign saying ":Entering rain forest" along the trail, and no need for one. You know at once that you are in no ordinary forest. Giant trees loft into the sky, hiding it from view, imperiously barring both sun and light from their domain. Beneath the canopy are more trees, many so tall that in another setting they too would stand out as colossi. High hanging gardens of moss soften the contours of branches; ferns spring out of trunks in midair. On the ground great carcasses of trees lie felled by storms and in various stages of returning to the soil; yet even as the logs rot, infant trees spring from them. More ferns and mosses decorate the forest floor, cushioning footfalls. The silence, like the greenness, is overwhelming. Even the rain that gives the forest its name falls noiselessly, absorbed by the spongy ground cover.

As scientists define it, a rain forest is a forest that receives at least 80 inches of rain a year. Such abundance is usually associated with the tropics, where winter is unknown and only two seasons prevail—one that is very wet, and another that is less wet. The combination of persistent downpour and constant warmth produces such jungles of lush green growth as the fabulous rain forest of the Amazon River Valley. In the Temperate Zone rain forests are a rarity, but the Olympic Peninsula boasts four of them: the Bogachiel and, in parallel river valleys running from the mountains to the ocean, the Hoh, the Queets and the Quinault. They not only meet but exceed the scientific standard of a rain forest. Though in a very dry July or August no more than an inch or two of rain may fall on them, the rest of the year makes up for it. As many as 40 inches of rain may fall in any winter month, and a total of 100 to 200 inches in an average year. The reason for this phenomenon lies in the vagaries of geography. All four valleys face west or southwest, and thus receive head-on the warm prevailing winds from across the Pacific. The winds encounter the mountains of the Olympic Range, are deflected upward, then quickly cool and unload their immense burden of moisture on the land, partly as snow on the mountaintops, partly as rain in the lowlands.

It takes a while for a visitor to the rain forest to sort out what seems at a glance to be an utter chaos of growth. There is, in fact, an orderly if complex structure to this plant society, composed of roughly horizontal strata. Tropical rain forests have as many as five such layers; the Bogachiel and other Olympic rain forests have three. In the Olympics the topmost layer is dominated by two kingly conifers, the Sitka spruce and the western hemlock, both of which may grow to a height of 200 feet or more. The Sitka spruce has an impressive girth as well; in some instances it would take the arm spreads of about a dozen men to encircle one of these trees at its base.

A simple but vital fact ensures the supremacy of the hemlock and the spruce in this environment: their total tolerance for shade when young. From the seedling stage on, they thrive in the muted light of the forest floor, a condition that spells doom for many other species. The hemlock and the spruce are the inch-high babies seen sprouting from fallen "nurse" logs; after a few years they send down roots that spraddle the log, probing earthward toward the mineral-rich soil they need. So tenacious is their hold that the tiny row they form atop the log when young becomes a stately colonnade in maturity, and their swollen bases outline the shape of the log centuries after the log itself has decomposed and disappeared.

Sharing the top story of the forest with the hemlock and the spruce are the Douglas fir and the western red cedar. But these splendid evergreens, which dominate many another forest on the Northwest coast, are here in a distinct minority. Sunlight is essential to their growth, and they are able to flourish in the rain forest only in the areas where fires or landslides or blowdowns of canopy trees have created patches of space open to the sky.

Beneath the conifers is a middle area of moss-laden deciduous trees, among them the big-leaf maple. This massive tree, with five-lobed leaves almost the size of platters, occasionally grows as high as 60 feet. It seems to be irresistibly attractive to graceful air plants, since it plays host to dozens of species. Another of the tree's guests, lovely but far less welcome, is the parasitic bracket fungus that protrudes from the bark. When I was young I used to break off pieces of the fungus and draw crude landscapes on their cream-colored undersides with a fingernail; after a day or two each etched line would turn a deep brown. I have learned since then that every tree that bears such a fungus is dead or dying, cancerously and fatally diseased.

The ground story of the rain forest is the most diversely tenanted, a profusion of young trees, berry bushes, vines, herbs, mosses and ferns. The vine maple, a spindly relative of the big-leaf maple, grows every which way, tangling with elderberry and salmonberry bushes. Beds of sword fern, deer fern and lady fern billow airily above a carpet of moss so thick in places that you sink into it ankle-deep. Here and there the pink of bedstraw, the yellow of the pioneer violet, the white of foamflower provide splashes of brightness to relieve the omnipresent green.

But flowers are few in this shaded realm. The moisture is what supplies the glitter. The rain, as it bounces down through the different forest layers, touches everything in its path; rarely does it miss the foliage and hit the ground at full force. Even the wind, which may be blowing hard over the top story, is usually diffused and gentled by the time it is felt on the forest floor.

The scene in a rain forest has been likened to green mansions, to a magical stage setting, to a hushed cathedral. It is, indeed, a place to walk softly and speak softly, no place to shout or to throw things. It is neither a lively place nor a dead one, though life and death are going on in every foot of it, in every leaf, in every hidden runway of a mole or shrew, in every cubic centimeter of cushiony plant matter under your feet. Perhaps that is what gives the rain forest a certain kind of eeriness, subduing yet not at all depressing. You are constantly aware that the busy forces of creation and decay are at work here exactly as they have been for many centuries.

Right now, sitting at my desk in a New York suburb, I feel the tug of a rain-forest memory, reaching across 3,000 miles to remind me of a private illusion. Sometimes, in one or another of these stately valleys, I have had a strange sense of being in a peaceable underwater grotto. Leaning against a stump and peering upward, I see patches of light through the quivering treetops 200 feet above and think: up there is the surface, not down here. The tall trees are spars of brown or green; fallen logs are submerged hulks, barnacled with moss. A squirrel and a downy woodpecker, skittering between branches, are darting fish. Except for them it is as quiet as at the bottom of the sea, and even the atmosphere is sea green. In a moment or two the illusion passes, and I take a deep breath, as if coming up for air.

Though some parts of the rain-forest understory are dense, like jungle, large areas are open and parklike—thanks to industrious browsing by the black-maned Roosevelt elk. The rain forests and all the rest of Olympic National Park are their official protectorate, and they freely wander the woods, singly or in herds of dozens, cropping the undergrowth, devouring even the appropriately named devil's-club, whose barbs are poisonously painful to man at the slightest touch. In the Hoh rain forest, the next south of the Bogachiel, I have seen old experimental enclosures that prove what a difference the elk make. Inside the wire fences, beyond the animals' reach, the vegetation is an impenetrable tangle. In the surrounding forest it is only knee-high.

Wings outspread and mouth open in a piercing croak, a raven uses a dead branch as a lookout. In the Olympic Peninsula, where it is a familiar sight, the raven favors open terrain but often scouts the forests for nuts, berries, mice and other small animals to satisfy its omnivorous appetite.

The elk came from Asia over the same busy Siberian land bridge that enabled mastodons and mammoths and the prehistoric ancestors of the Indians to cross into the Americas. For thousands of years the elk roamed the entire length of the coastal forests, but the largest surviving population, some 12,000 to 14,000, lives on the Olympic Peninsula. As many as 5,000 elk now reside inside the boundaries of the park. Many never leave the rain forests, although some herds migrate up the valleys to the cooler mountain meadows for the summer.

They are the biggest land mammal of the Northwest coast and, next to the moose, the biggest species in the deer family; a full-grown bull may weigh half a ton. Bull or cow, the elk starts out as a 30-pound weakling, born in May or June as the offspring of autumnal mating. It is tawny at birth, spotted for better camouflage; for a while it lies curled up, getting used to being alive, then it struggles to its feet in a few hours. It stays close to its mother for its first summer, though if the family is migrating to alpine meadows it must shift for itself on the month-long journey, following steep, faint trails and fording swift streams where a slip may break a leg and bring on a predator. Its father is no help, for the bulls have headed for the high hills a fortnight ahead of the cows and new calves.

An inexplicable thing happens when the migrants reach the end of their trip at some snow-banked mountain basin. With complete abandon, young and old suddenly break into a dance, a wild revel of prancing and pawing that goes on until the creatures drop from exhaustion. When they have calmed down and rested, an idyllic summer lies ahead, with grasses and herbs for browsing and snow patches for snoozing (for relief not only from the heat but also from the fleas).

The idyll ends in early fall when the urge to mate strikes the bulls. Older males rejoin the herd first, rounding up harems of cows. Then the bachelor bulls and younger but sexually mature males of two or three years start to move in on the herd bulls. All the bulls have been preparing for combat, practicing their jousting and polishing the tines of their antlers against trees, rubbing off the antlers' summer velvet. The challenger voices his intention with a loud, shrill bugling, sometimes accompanied by a low, ominous vibrato. I have heard this battle cry echoing through ridges and canyons, and it is as chilling as the trumpet call of a rampaging elephant. The challenged bull bugles back as he shepherds his harem to a sheltered hillside and awaits the attack. A young, callow challenger approaches as close as he dares, then usually feints and falls back. A real challenger comes on deliberately and menacingly. No longer wasting breath on bellowing, he and the herd bull circle each other warily, then close in to jab savagely with antlers and strike out with lightning-swift slashes of hoofs. The combatants may lock horns, snorting and glaring in a titanic tug of war; once in a great while they cannot break loose and stay interlocked, doomed to die together, not of exhaustion but of starvation. Some battles end when one bull is killed, but most are resolved when one contestant gives up and sullenly walks away. Often the victor finds he has gained an empty victory, for when he looks around he sees that other, shrewder bulls have made off with his prospective wives while he was fighting for them.

At one time the voracious Olympic wolf made life hazardous for the elk, but woodsmen exterminated the wolves: nobody has seen one in 50 years. Bears, which will eat anything including carrion of their own kind, have never been much of a threat, being too slow and lazy to catch a healthy elk, and besides the rain forests are so full of berries and beetles that the bears rarely go hungry. A more formidable enemy of the elk is the cougar. The biggest cat in North America—variously called mountain lion, puma, panther and *Felis concolor hippolestes, hippolestes* meaning horse-killer—the cougar grows to more than six feet in length and to 175 pounds, and can propel itself 20 feet through the air in a single bound. A frightened elk can run 35 miles an hour, but not forever; furthermore, it runs with head held high and antlers laid back to avoid their being snapped off by trees. In this position, an elk is no match for a cougar crouched on a limb overhead, waiting to spring.

In the period when the elk's-tooth charm was in fashion it was man who endangered the species; hunters left thousands of dead, toothless elk throughout the Olympic Peninsula. And by a kind of poetic justice it was man who gave the elk a new lease on life—specifically, two men who were also Presidents of the United States.

The first was Theodore Roosevelt, who had stalked more than his share of elk in the Rockies. This species, named *wapiti* by the Shoshone Indians, is smaller and lighter colored than the Olympic species; it still survives in the Rockies. In 1897 the great naturalist C. Hart Merriam described "a new elk from the Olympics," adding, "I deem it a privilege to name this splendid animal Roosevelt's wapiti." T.R., in whom the manly hunter and the tender conservationist were always somewhat at odds, was pleased at the honor, and kept it in mind throughout the years of his Presidency. Two days before leaving office in 1909, he put his name to a proclamation setting aside about 600,000 acres of

Winter's rime ice, formed by moist Pacific air hitting cold tree trunks, coats the windward side of firs at timberline on Hurricane Ridge.

the Olympic National Forest as the Mount Olympus National Monument. Though hunting—and logging as well—were still permitted in the forest, the monument was henceforth to be a last refuge for his namesake. The Roosevelt elk, T.R. declared, was the "noblest of the stag kind throughout the world . . . whoever kills him has killed the chief of his race."

Twenty-nine years later President Franklin D. Roosevelt made the protectorate more secure, signing a bill that locked up—from the saw as well as the gun—nearly a million acres of land, including the monument, as Olympic National Park. Before deciding on this move, F.D.R. went out to see the place for himself. I was along as a member of the press party when his motorcade toured the Olympic Peninsula. He sat up late one night at Lake Crescent to hear arguments for and against a park. Officials of the Forest Service, which traditionally had managed the area, told him the move would be an economic disaster, a waste of good, ripe timber; they assured the President they could look out for the elk as well as the National Park Service could. "But I think we antagonized him," one official later told me. Next day the President sat on the veranda of the lodge at Lake Quinault. He said nothing; he simply stared out toward the mountains that shield the Enchanted Valley and its lovely waterfalls deep in the peninsula's interior. Back in Washington, Roosevelt pressed Congress to establish the kind of protected national park he wanted—the biggest anyone had yet dared to propose for the peninsula.

Before that time and since, the Olympic wilderness has been more fought over than any other in the country. Amid some hue and cry in World War I, President Wilson halved the size of the monument set aside by the first Roosevelt on the ground that its Sitka spruce was needed for airplanes. The war ended before much spruce was cut. In World War II, lumbermen again sought to log the spruce, again for wartime needs; Interior Secretary Harold Ickes told them to find the spruce elsewhere. Periodically since then, campaigns have been mounted to shrink the park by a fifth to a half, for a gamut of reasons: to ease a housing shortage or a job shortage, to check a tree disease, to keep lumber mills supplied, to make the woods accessible to the millions who drive rather than to the few who backpack. Up to now the campaigns have been of no avail. The only trees that may be felled in the park are those considered a danger on the trails.

In the Olympic National Forest, which surrounds the park on three sides, the story is very different. Clear-cutting—removing all the trees from a tract of forest and leaving only slash and rubble—goes on apace. Vast patches of woodland, on gentle slopes and steep ones, offer an instant affront to the eye; they have been scalped by a process not unlike strip-mining. In the aftermath some are regenerating with young trees and some are not.

Clear-cutting has obvious advantages for the logger. He needs to go into the tract only once to get out the trees, and he doesn't have to waste time being selective; but no matter how efficient or desirable the process is from the logger's point of view, one thing is clear: what he leaves behind is no longer wilderness. One day, just outside the park, I followed an empty logging truck up a mountainside in the valley of the Hoh, curious to see where it would go. It was going back for more, and I figured that if the truck could climb the steepest grades I had ever driven, so could my station wagon. It was a well-made crushed-rock road, dizzying when I looked down over the side into the valley, and at its end a bulldozer was clinging to a hillside, extending the road through the trees along even steeper slopes. Even as the road was still being built, a diesel-powered winch was snaking fresh, fragrant logs up to where a giant crane was loading them like so many toothpicks onto waiting trucks. On this naked, scarified ground, where the soil would wash downslope in the next heavy rainfall, not a single plant big enough to be called a tree was left growing and not a creature was stirring; and it would be a long time before anything did.

On another day, my wife and I viewed the corpse of a coastal forest a few miles to the west, on a long drive through the Quinault Indian Reservation. As Indian tribes go, the Quinaults were left relatively well off by the white man's take-over of the West. They had the biggest reservation in western Washington, a triangle whose base was 27 miles of unspoiled coastline and whose apex was at Lake Quinault, 30 miles inland. Inside the triangle was a vast and variegated stand of conifers, abutting the Quinault rain forest to the east and containing a rich mix of Sitka spruce, western red cedar, western hemlock, Douglas fir and Pacific silver fir. Winding through the reservation were one big river, the twisting Quinault, up which the salmon and steelhead surged every year, and hundreds of smaller tributary streams where the fish turned off to spawn. Along miles of the ocean beach, millions of razor clams were bedded down.

The beach is still there, though the Quinaults have had to close it to outsiders to keep it clean. The forest is mostly gone, four fifths of it having been clear-cut under contracts let by the Bureau of Indian Affairs. Along with it most of the fish have disappeared. Accompanied by Guy McMinds, a fisheries biologist and director of resource and development for the tribal council, my wife and I crisscrossed the reservation over miles of one-lane logging roads. Without Guy's sense of direction we quickly would have become lost, for the maze of roads is marked only with timber-company and Bureau of Indian Affairs code numbers. For long stretches the roads are dusty green tunnels. A fringe of red alder and vine maple forms the walls, interlacing overhead. Countless speeding logging trucks have clipped the branches so that the tunnels, in profile, have the same high ovaloid shape as a loaded truck.

Beyond this fringe is desolation. The loggers have taken the cream of the crop. The slashings are strewn over the landscape as far as you can see, like the wreckage left in the wake of a tornado. The spawning streams, still trickling with tea-colored water from the tannin in the wood, are jammed everywhere with discarded, whitening trees. A rabbit might negotiate this clogged terrain, but no elk or deer or bear could get through. And young trees are scarce; 15 years after logging there is no sign of forest regeneration.

The logging of the reservation's wilderness was not accomplished without the compliance of some Quinaults, who got more money for their timber birthright than they had ever seen. But it impoverished the tribe. Belatedly in 1971, the Indians barricaded their roads to the trucks of the Aloha Lumber Corporation and I.T.T. Rayonier, seeking to force the loggers and the Bureau of Indian Affairs to clean up the mess and start replanting the forest. A federal court injunction soon put a stop to that dramatic confrontation and the logging resumed, though a few of the choked streams have since been cleared. The Quinaults have been resourceful in coping with catastrophe; they have a dozen rehabilitation projects underway, from fish hatcheries and clam canneries to timber-salvage operations on thousands of acres of slashings left by the clear-cutters.

"In my lifetime," said Guy McMinds, "we may very well see the salmon runs come back. But we won't live long enough to see our wilderness forest come back."

The prediction seemed almost too gloomy, yet a haunting picture flashed through my mind of a place Roger Allin had pointed out to me toward the end of our Bogachiel trip. It was a patch of flatland, now part of Olympic National Park, that had been logged long before the present park boundaries were drawn. Stumps of Sitka spruce reared on all sides like huge goblins. Some were six, others eight feet tall; these were the heights at which men had once stood on springboards to saw through the trunks. In those free-and-easy days it had been simpler and quicker to cut a tree well above its base, where the trunk began to taper. Leaving a stump eight feet high didn't matter, because there were plenty of other trees to cut. In the decades since the law put a stop to logging operations inside the park, an alder thicket had sprung up, mixed with some scraggly firs—but the majestic Sitka spruce at the site have never come back.

Thinking of that scene, and of Guy McMinds' pessimism about his beloved coastal forest, I find it hard to avoid a sense of foreboding about the future of the great evergreen belt that once adorned the Olympic Peninsula so magnificently. There is, to be sure, an occasional ray of hope. One is the fact that a few lumber companies have abandoned the industry's historic cut-and-run policy. They intend to stay in business forever. On the public lands they clear-cut, they pursue the practice of quick reforestation, two or three times if the initial replanting does not take hold; on their own private lands the firms increasingly pursue the practice of thinning out the trees, thus allowing the remaining stands to grow faster and taller.

But the attitude of these companies is not typical of the industry, and the classic confrontation persists between people who feel it is a sin to let a mature and merchantable tree stand, and people who feel it is a sin to cut it down. For those of us who prefer never to take the sanctity of wilderness for granted, the price of wilderness—like the price of liberty—would seem to be eternal vigilance.

The Restless Forest

PHOTOGRAPHS BY TOM TRACY

"Who can impress the forest, bid the tree/ Unfix his earth-bound root?" So Macbeth jubilantly exclaimed when told that Birnam Wood must move up Dunsinane hill before he could be vanquished. Yet as every reader of Shakespeare knows, eventually Birnam Wood did come to Dunsinane. Other forests move too, not by uprooting themselves and marching, but by spreading over areas where no forest grew before. This process is called forest succession, and one of its most dramatic instances is evident in the western Olympics, in the nearly parallel valleys of the Hoh, Queets and Quinault rivers.

The floors of these U-shaped valleys are as much as three quarters of a mile wide, along which the shallow rivers meander in wide loops. Often a river will change course, particularly during spring floods, and leave behind a soggy patch of land that was the riverbed. This is the incubator of a forest to come. In about 1,000 years, the bare surface will have turned into a thick forest of towering trees, springy mosses and a revel of tangled plants.

The cycle of forest growth in these valleys is slow, continuous and sometimes overlapping, but it can be roughly divided into four recogniz-able stages. During the first stage, grasses and willows grow in the thin, gravelly soil and are soon followed by alders. In the second stage, bigger deciduous trees such as cottonwoods and maples, as well as the evergreen spruces, shade out the alders. Young hemlocks, too, begin to appear. As the trees start to crowd one another, the forest gradually thins its ranks to spruce and hemlock and, finally, to the more shade tolerant of the two, hemlock. The forest has now reached its permanent, or climax, stage. Barring external interference, no other trees will crowd out the hemlocks.

No man can stand on a gravel bank and wait for a forest to grow around him. But each stage of forest succession can be seen by simply walking away from the river, up the sloping floor of the Hoh, Queets or Quinault valley. Since the time they were formed by glaciers and then eroded by the river, parts of the valleys have already been through forest succession or are in one or another of its stages. To walk up from the river level is thus to move backward through the forest generations. But it is also a move forward in time, a preview of what the future holds for the now barren river bars below.

In the southwest of Olympic National Park, the Queets Valley lies under a patchwork mantle of trees that marks various stages in forest succession. Alder woods border sandy gravel bars, while elsewhere in the valley clumps of maples and cottonwoods form bright green slashes next to darker, denser spruce and hemlock stands.

A gravel bar begins its conversion to a forest. At right, willows and alders have taken hold; in the background, an alder stand flourishes.

The First Stage: from Pebbles to Alders

When a river changes its course, its abandoned bed is exposed as a damp surface of gravel and cobbles called a gravel bar. A luxuriant forest will someday cover this barren scene, but the first fuzz of growth is meager: velvet grass, sedge, sheep's sorrel, western millet and sturdy strawberry plants. Soon clumps of lithe willow trees will spring up from among the pebbles, though they are more shrubs than trees.

However sparse this early vegetation, it works persistently to prepare the gravel bar for more plant life. The grasses form mats, and the willows' roots trap silt from the water. Spring floods bring more sand. In a few years, the area is ready for its first trees—slender red alders whose shallow roots allow them to grow in thin soil. The alders prepare the soil for the future forest in their own way, by enriching it with nitrogen. Pure nitrogen is abundant in the air, but few plants can absorb it directly. By means of bacteria in their roots, alders draw nitrogen from air in the soil and convert it to nitrogen compounds. The trees' decomposing leaves and wood return these compounds to the soil in a form other plants can use.

A community of alders may take 15 to 20 years to form and will dominate its patch of land for another 40 to 50 years. But by then other trees, taking root in the now richer, deeper soil, will have come to challenge the alders' sovereignty.

Flooded but thriving, a lone willow glistens in the rain.

Strawberry plants creep among a gravel bar's cobbles.

The Second Stage: a Mixed Community

In a part of the valley 10 feet higher than the river level, on land that was a gravel bar 300 years ago, the second stage of forest succession progresses. Often, as seen in the picture at right, there is a sharp delineation, almost a platform, between this stage and the alders at the water's edge. In this more elevated area cohabit various species of trees: black cottonwoods, maples, Sitka spruces and some western hemlocks. But willows and alders are conspicuously absent—the bigger trees have already shaded them out.

In the rich soil of this area, trees grow to generous proportions. The black cottonwood, whose dark green leaves turn silvery-white undersides to the wind, reaches 125 feet. Sitka spruce, the largest of all spruces, from 150 to 200 feet tall, boasts diameters of four to six feet. The big-leaf maple sometimes spreads its branches as wide as it is high—60 feet—but its distinguishing feature is its five-lobed leaf, which can be as much as 15 inches across. A few western hemlocks, forerunners of the climax forest, appear here and there, hinting at the evergreen grandeur to come.

This dynamic society of compatible trees will flourish for about 500 years, but the growing profusion of leaves and spreading branches will gradually thicken the high canopy and inexorably shut out the sun. Eventually the changing conditions will dictate a change in the forest.

A few feet above a backwater bordered by red alders, a level terrace supports the second-

stage forest growth. Most of the trees in this raised, sunlit area are big-leaf maples, but a clump of spruce stands at right, casting a deep shade.

Two hundred feet straight up, spruce and hemlock mingle their branches, threatening to shade out the maples at a lower level.

The Third Stage: the Rain Forest

Moist, lush, almost tropical in its profusion of growth, the third stage of forest succession is the multilayered community commonly known as the rain forest. In this area, which is from 15 to 20 feet above the river level, Sitka spruce and western hemlock dominate—and compete. Since both evergreens grow to 200 feet or more, they have equal access to the open sky, and the stiff, spiky needles of the spruce vie for sunlight with the rounded and glossy needles of the hemlock's drooping branches.

Despite their preeminent position, these trees do not prevent a mob of plants from growing beneath them. Occasional big-leaf maples stoop in the shade, heavily draped with moss. A little lower, trailing shrubs tangle with high ferns. Serpentine vine maples grow to heights of 35 feet after creeping along on the ground around trunks and under logs. Mosses cushion the floor, along with delicate ground covers such as the three-petaled trillium and the droopy Oregon oxalis. Logs lie among the plants in various stages of decay. These rotting logs are vital to the health of the forest. They not only replenish the soil, but also serve as nurse logs to seedlings, providing them with moisture and nourishment for several years, until as saplings they gain a foothold in the soil.

The third forest stage lasts about 300 years, but as the shade grows more dense, even the spruce trees gradually bow out to the hemlocks.

Draping the sturdy limbs of a big-leaf maple, bunches of club moss hang in ragged fringes.

Next to a thick spruce trunk, a sinewy vine maple basks in a temporary ray of sunlight.

112/

Blossoms of Oregon oxalis, a leafy ground cover, droop under drops of rain water.

Their petals collared by three slender leaves, trilliums sprout from the mossy ground.

Rising in rows atop decaying logs, spruce and hemlock

trees form a colonnade through a dim glade. Once tiny seedlings nourished by these nurse logs, the trees are now firmly rooted in the soil.

The Fourth Stage: the Climax Forest

Insofar as there is permanence anywhere in the plant world, it can be found in the climax forests of the Hoh, Queets and Quinault valleys. Here, 60 feet above river level, is the final stage of forest succession. In this community, which if undisturbed will perpetuate itself indefinitely, western hemlock outnumbers the spruce four to one, thanks to the hemlock's greater shade tolerance and more viable seeds. The seeds can lie for years waiting for the right conditions in which to germinate, whereas spruce seeds soon lose their vitality. Once sown, hemlock seedlings grow vigorously in shade that spruce seedlings find uncongenial.

The big-leaf and vine maples and other deciduous trees are missing from this somber forest. Now only ground covers and shrubs remain, growing thickly in the rich, moist soil, and making the most of rare streaks of sunlight.

As the climax stage, the hemlock forest would someday take over the whole valley, right down to the river's edge, if conditions remained the same. But anything from fire to drought to man's meddling could interrupt the orderly succession. And the river itself may prove the greatest threat to the dominance of the hemlocks, undercutting trees and carrying away soil as it shifts course. The old riverbed will be left behind as a denuded gravel bar—and there, the whole cycle of forest succession will begin once more.

Aristocrats of forest succession, lofty hemlocks rule a hillside of the Hoh Valley. Amid th

und cover in the patch of sunlight at right, a new generation of hemlock seedlings prepares to join the community it will help perpetuate.

5/ Fresh Waters and Fish Stories

*Every time a rosy, shining steelhead leaped near the
boat...I felt grateful to him for showing the joy of life,
the need of a fish to play and have a fleeting moment out of
his natural element.* ZANE GREY/ AT THE MOUTH OF THE KLAMATH

Quilcene and Quinault, Queets and Quillayute, Hamma Hamma and
Hoh, Klaskanine and Klamath, Duckabush and Dosewallips and Dungeness: the names of the rivers that pour fresh water into salt along the
Northwest coast are an Indian litany that rolls off the tongue like an incantation to so many gods. All of them are the white man's phonetic ap-
proximations, for the Indians never had a written language. The whites
themselves christened the numberless creeks that feed the rivers, and
while they were linguistically resourceful they were hardly poetic: Hee
Hee, Hee Haw, Jimmiecomelately, Three Prune, Promise, Success and
One Too Many are among hundreds of enigmatic creek names that
have outlived their authors.

Inelegantly named or not, rivers great and small follow labyrinthine
paths through the whole coastal region between Vancouver Island and
southern Oregon. The Columbia River, the major river system, rises in
western Canada's remote highlands and meanders 1,200 miles to the Pacific, from which every drop of its water originally was drawn up into
clouds and carried inland in the earth's endless, life-giving water cycle.
The atmosphere sucks up moisture by evaporation from the ocean and
by transpiration from the trees; rain and snow descend from the clouds;
rivers then return the water to its source.

Far smaller than the Columbia, but moderately long nonetheless, are
such rivers as the Willamette, the Rogue and the Umpqua. They seek

their outlets along the coast, but they all originate in the Cascades to the east. The rivers that are most characteristic of the Northwest coast are the many short ones that generally travel no more than 15 miles from start to finish. The mouths of some of these rivers are almost within sight of their headwaters, so close are the mountains to the shore.

Most of these waterways are born in high snowfields and glacial run-offs, moving with noisy urgency as they plunge through mountain gorges. Those that originate in the Olympic Range do something else as well. Because the range tends to get higher toward the center of the peninsula, the rivers tumble down in a radial pattern. They also tend to curve during their descent, so that trying to follow a stream bed can be tricky for the hiker in the mountains. I was warned that if I were ever lost I should stay on the ridges, where I could see where I was going, and not be guided by a stream, which would almost certainly change direction and could lead to box canyons and torrential waterfalls. Thus far, I am glad to say, I have not had to test the advice.

Once on the lowlands, the rivers slow down, and the smoothed stones on their bottoms become covered with talcum-fine, dove-gray "glacier powder"—silt ground from ancient rocks—as the shallow stream beds spread out in twisted braids through the forested valleys. Finally the waters turn green and placid, pocked with resting holes for fish, as they glide to sea level.

The lakes of the Northwest coast, like the rivers, come in almost every imaginable size and shape: high-level, low-level, long and narrow, broad and seemingly bottomless. Some nestle high in the mountains, others nearly merge with the sea. Along the Oregon shore are lakes so close to the ocean that, viewing them from a plane, one might imagine they were outsized tidal pools. However, these are fresh-water lakes, some as long as 10 miles, others only a fraction of a mile. Eons ago they were salty, in an area inundated by a rising sea. Sand-bars, spits and dunes closed off the water-filled lowlands, and rain as well as streams from the mountains eventually altered the trapped water from salt to brackish to fresh. The lakes might have become bays, except that their sluggish waters lacked the force to cut permanent channels through the sand barriers separating them from the sea, which in places is only hundreds of yards away. Some of these barriers are in fact quite formidable: the fresh water of Lake Cleawox, just south of Florence, is separated from the Pacific by dunes as high as 160 feet.

To the north in Washington, the Olympic Peninsula has almost 1,000 lakes and ponds of its own—many with no outlets to lead their waters oceanward. Typical of these are the clear, bright blue mountain tarns in little basins scooped out long ago by glaciers: they fill up when the snow melts on the surrounding slopes, then shrink by evaporation in late summer, when the uplands burst into flower. In winter the lakes freeze, looking like little patches of snow-white carpeting drawn taut.

But of all the lakes in the Olympics, Lake Crescent, on the northern side of the peninsula, is the one I love best. It is nine miles long and only vaguely crescent shaped, filling an irregular and very deep hollow excavated by glaciers. The last time I saw it was on an Indian summer day, and for the first time in all my visits there was not the shadow of a cloud on its countenance. The rugged hills that rear steeply from its northern and eastern shores were affable in warm sunlight. The lake is seldom so benign; more often it is forbidding, darkened to steel blue by the mountains' shadows. Even in repose it seems braced for some catastrophe. And catastrophes do come, with scant warning: terrifying storms that send thunderclaps cannonading off Storm King and Sourdough mountains, while wild winds whip the water into froth and sometimes topple great trees in a Götterdämmerung of sound and fury.

I cannot remember my earliest trip to Lake Crescent because I was several months from being born when my mother and father discovered it for themselves. She was 22 and he was 26; they drove as close as they could by touring car and rode the rest of the way on horseback. I can only imagine their feelings as they rounded a bend in the hills and came suddenly upon that vast, dark and silent mass of water cupped by glowering mountains. Whatever the lake's temper that day, its rough-cut beauty must have made them pull up and stare.

Black-visaged and scary as it was and usually still is, Lake Crescent had an attraction that called my parents back, year after year, until I was 12. There was a little car ferry that crossed the lake to a rustic camp called Rosemary, where we always stayed. It was a hideaway never shared with our friends in town, a Brothers Grimm setting whose woods and water alike were too deep to explore very far. We always did our swimming close to the sandy shore because we had been warned that the lake was bottomless.

From my father's rowboat, trolling the lake, we learned to fish. Those were the days before man had brought his pollutants to the Northwest coast, and we had an almost unlimited choice of easy fish to catch —such as cutthroat or whitefish—but under my father's tutelage we soon learned that a real prize was a rainbow trout or a steelhead or,

A black bear sits on a grassy slope in the Olympic foothills. With an appetite for anything from salmon to rodents to berries, the bears find the area a rich hunting ground, and prosper accordingly—more than 200 of them live in Olympic National Park itself.

above all, a salmon. It was from my father that we first heard of the mysterious ways of this incredible fish that spawned in the streams of the Northwest. We never ceased to be fascinated with his tales of their epic round-trip journeys from tiny creek to open ocean and back again, after six months to six years at sea—to the very same spot, unerringly. It still is not known how the salmon find their way home so precisely; one theory holds that they are guided by the distinctive smell of the waters. In any event, we children were content with the mystery. Salmon are traditionally the pride of the Northwest, and by absorbing the stories of their exploits we somehow shared in that pride.

There are five species of Pacific salmon, and all five were identified as far back as 1741 by the German naturalist Georg Wilhelm Steller, the man for whom the Steller sea lions of the Northwest coast were named. This remarkable scientist accompanied Vitus Bering on an expedition for the Russians, and made extensive observations of marine life along the eastern Pacific. Steller classified the five species of salmon he studied in the genus *Oncorhynchus* (for hook-nosed). The common names for the species vary from town to town and even from person to person. In average sizes they range from the four-pound pink, or humpback, salmon to the 25-pound king, or Chinook. In between are the coho, or silver, salmon; the chum, or keta or dog, salmon; and the blueback, or sockeye—sometimes also called the Quinault, after one of its favorite spawning lakes; it is the only one that seems to prefer a lake to a stream for spawning. But the average sizes I have cited should not be taken as gospel. In the case of Chinooks, for example, specimens of 100 pounds—and five feet long—are in the record books.

The salmon and its streamlined relative the steelhead, which may grow to 45 pounds, are anadromous fish—they must come back in from the ocean and go upstream to spawn. But where the steelhead may spawn several times in a lifetime, the salmon spawn just once and then die. The female salmon, swimming against the current, vigorously scoops out her nest—called a redd—in the gravel of the stream bed with her tail and body, then voids a stream of eggs into it—anywhere from 2,000 to 6,000. The male, hovering beside her in the water, ejects milt that sinks to envelop and fertilize the eggs. The parents then cover the eggs with gravel and move off, weakening as they go and finally unable to swim at all. Both die within a few days of the spawning.

Salmon, and steelhead as well, are beset by nonhuman predators from the moment of birth to the moment of death. A merganser swooping down on a river pool may scoop up a dozen infant fish in one mouthful. And once the young venture out to sea, where they spend most of their lives, every bigger fish or mammal poses a threat. Back at the rivers on the spawning journey, birds of prey lurk, along with mink and otters—and black bears. When salmon are spawning, the black bears change their usual diet of small rodents, berries, beetles and skunk cabbage and go fishing. Being indolent by nature, they prefer a salmon exhausted after the effort of spawning. But often a bear will snatch a still-vigorous salmon from the water, break its back with a bite or a paw-swipe, and tote it ashore to eat at leisure.

For all their voracious appetites, the black bears have never endangered any entire species of salmon, any more than the Indians did. What has endangered the fish, and in some areas wiped out their runs, has been civilized man's penchant for overfishing, damming and dumping. Grand Coulee and other dams ended the upper Columbia's function as a broad freeway to the salmon-spawning creeks. The Willamette River, which joins the Columbia at Portland, through the years turned into a spillway of industrial wastes. Oregonians woke up just in time. In the past few years the Willamette has revived. It is once again swimmable—if not drinkable—and once again habitable for salmon.

Fortunately for the fish and the wildlife they help sustain, many other rivers of the Northwest coast are still relatively unspoiled. Even today there are few dams—and no high ones—on the Olympic Peninsula, and a salmon or steelhead that survives to return homeward has a fair chance of getting up an unimpeded stream to spawn.

In the northern Olympics, the Dungeness River, where it comes out of the dense woods a few miles inland, is impeded not by dams or debris but by a simple "salmon rack"—a flat grille of two-inch vertical planks anchored by stout tripods driven into the riverbed. The rack was built by Ernest Brannon, who runs the nearby state fish hatchery, as a trap where he could intercept salmon to strip them of their eggs and milt. One late-summer day, when the river's flow barely washed over the planking, Ernie and I stood beside it. He was getting ready to catch fish and had strung a five-foot-high wire netting across the 65-foot breadth of the stream. "Without that, they'd jump right over," he said, "hard enough to knock a man down if he had his back turned." In the deep water below the rack we could see dark, yard-long shapes moving about like restless toy submarines. They were Chinook salmon, balked in their upstream migration by the barrier.

The hundreds of thousands of salmon eggs that Ernie garners are fer-

Sockeye salmon, both silvery females and gaudy

males, head up an Olympic stream to spawn where they were born four to six years before. Mission accomplished, they will die within 10 days.

tilized and hatched in indoor tanks; the resulting small fry swim about in outdoor pools, thriving on pellets of enriched food, safer and better nourished than they would be at their natural spawning grounds upstream. Later, as fingerlings, they are transported to a pair of big artificial ponds that Brannon has built at Hurd Creek down the Dungeness, from which they can easily swim to the nearby salt water. Four, five, even six years later the survivors return to the river as full-grown Chinooks, and the life cycle begins all over again.

Ernie Brannon raises his salmon so that there will be an adequate supply of Chinooks for commercial fishermen and for the likes of me, the occasional sport fisherman. It is partly thanks to Brannon that the Chinook has not been edged toward oblivion—and it was perhaps thanks to some other hatcheryman that I once caught a really big one.

One beautiful summer day I was fishing with my father in Puget Sound. Trolling in those waters as he did almost every day, he had boated many a king salmon, as he called the Chinook; but I, a transplanted Westerner returning from New York, had never caught a one. I was old enough to call my father Charlie, and young enough to be intimidated by his lifelong fishing proficiency. Sun glinted off the gray-green water, pebbled beaches shone white and clean, fir trees were blackish green against the sky. For hours nothing happened.

A friend named Bob Mills, fishing alone, came alongside and said to me, "Why don't you hop in my boat and maybe change your luck?" I stepped from Charlie's boat into Bob's and two minutes later there was a tremendous tug on my line that said a fish had struck. For three quarters of an hour we kept up a tug of war, until both the fish and I were exhausted. Almost docile, it swam toward the boat and suddenly was alongside. I reached for my net but before I could dip it into the water, the salmon rolled over, rising almost lazily—and the hook came free. In a moment the fish too would realize that it was free, and be off. But over my shoulder Bob's arm flashed down as he gaffed the fish with one sure stroke. From his boat nearby Charlie looked at us, his face a mixture of gladness for me and regret for himself, but when we held up the fish he had to remove his cigar and smile. At 40 pounds, 12 ounces, a pound for every inch of its length, mine—*mine*—was the biggest king salmon taken that season at that place.

But my triumph that day could never match my father's when he battled and bested a Beardslee trout—Lake Crescent's most famous fish. Some people doubt that the Beardslee, like the denizen of Loch Ness, even exists; others know it exists, but argue about what it is. One theory holds that it is a hybrid of a rainbow trout and something else. I got an expert's opinion from Dr. Lauren Donaldson, professor of fisheries at the University of Washington. Dr. Donaldson says the Beardslee is not a separate species or even a subspecies; it is, though, a distinct race of trout that evolved in the isolation of Lake Crescent after being trapped by some prehistoric landslide that blocked its exit stream. "If you want to catch one," he advised me, "fish at the thermocline, the level about 60 feet down where the cold, oxygen-poor bottom waters intersect with the warmer, better-aerated surface waters."

In 1922, writing in *Western Out-of-Doors,* E. B. Webster called the Beardslee "the hardest fighting fish, the gamest fish, in all the world. . . . Frequently a big one [up to 23 pounds] will fight a full two hours before being brought to net." I submit that this is a grand fish story—and I believe every word of it. The fish that Webster extolled got its name from Rear Admiral Lester Anthony Beardslee, U.S.N., who in 1895 anchored his flagship, the cruiser *Philadelphia,* at Port Angeles and made a successful fishing trip on horseback to Lake Crescent. Puzzled by his catch and not knowing whether he had boated a variant of the rainbow or steelhead or a landlocked salmon, the admiral sent several of the fish by courier down to David Starr Jordan, president of Stanford University and an ichthyologist of note. After close study, Dr. Jordan reported that the specimens differed from all forms of trout or steelhead he had ever seen. He graciously classified the admiral's find as a subspecies in its own right, and named it *Salmo gairdneri beardsleei.*

My father's luck was seldom as good as Admiral Beardslee's: he considered it a highly successful season if he caught one Beardslee. Daybreak after daybreak would find him out on the lake, barely visible from shore through mountain shadow or pelting rain, grimly rowing, and towing at depth the hand-made silver spoon that was reputed to be the one and only lure a Beardslee might take. At the end of our summer at the lake, if he had hauled in one Beardslee, he would sing to himself and to us all the way back home to Seattle. After a trip when he had failed, it was gloom all the way, and you could tell something was bothering him. But another summer brought another challenge and another chance—at Lake Crescent and its famous fish.

6/ Creatures of the Coast

---

*Here too is life, life with the resilient strength
of flesh and blood, fur and feathers, bone and shell
and plant tissue.*   DON GREAME KELLEY/ *EDGE OF A CONTINENT*

The pursuit began on a Pacific Ocean beach when I noticed a demure little dimple in the sand—the telltale "show" of a razor clam. Being hungry, I thought why not go after it? A stick of driftwood was handy, and with my back to the surf I began excavating, six inches seaward from the dimple so as not to break the clam shell. (The razor clam keeps its back, or hinged side, to the sea, protecting its razor-sharp ventral side.) The sand was wet and the digging hard but the hole was soon armpit deep. My fingertips touched something rubbery, the clam's siphon, and something smooth and hard, its retreating shell. I touched it, but that was all. Equipped with a strong digging "foot" that enables it to jack itself down, the clam was faster than I was. The tide was coming in, the hole was filling with water, and the only way to dig deeper was to submerge my head. I moved the sand back in place and headed, all drippy and gritty, for higher ground.

Fifty miles from the coast on another shoreline on another day I had better luck with a geoduck (pronounced *gooey-duck*), the giant among western clams. Prowling a calm Hood Canal beach during an unusually low tide, and armed this time with a small spade, I saw a foot-high jet of water spurt out of the sand just ahead. I knew I could dig at leisure this time, for the atrophied digging foot of the grown geoduck is almost as useless as the human appendix. Wherever the geoduck happens to settle down in its larval stage and grow up, that is where it will be stuck for life, buried anywhere from 18 inches to six feet in sand and mud. This one was only a couple of feet down and an easy mark. It kept retracting its siphon, nearly as fat as a baseball bat, but in 10 minutes it was mine. Grasped in my two hands, it came out of the muck with a sucking sound and squirted me in the eye. It was eminently keepable, about four pounds, with a shell eight inches long and a siphon that protruded eight inches more, even after it had been pulled as far in as the clam could pull it.

I would be stretching the truth to say I spent that evening pondering the differences in the life styles and habitats of the agile razor clam, which thrives in turbulent surf, and the immobilized geoduck, which requires a placid bottom. I simply sliced off, pounded and fried two geoduck steaks, saved the neck to chop for chowder, and went to bed feeling self-satisfied and well fed. But I have thought a lot since then about this saline world and its inhabitants, from the microscopic, all-but-weightless plant-animals that cloud the water to the multiton whales that barge through it.

The Northwest coast is not one kind of seacoast but two. There is the ocean strip, a stretch of 600 miles that directly confronts the Pacific and is at the mercy of its not always pacific moods. And there are the thousands of meandering miles of shore that reach inland from the Pacific by way of the Strait of Juan de Fuca, Puget Sound and Hood Canal. This shoreline is nourished, but not fiercely punished, by the sea; most of the year the biggest waves come in the wake of boats. The western shoreline, by contrast, is one long battle line, where far-traveled ocean waves strike the land with a force seldom exceeded elsewhere in the Northern Hemisphere, exploding bits of rock out of sheer cliffs and washing away trees and the crumbly stone-and-soil conglomerate of sloping banks. The assault is endless. Yet not many miles away, on the sheltered inland sea, the quarrying and abrading forces of geology seem to have slowed almost to a stop. The same tides come and go and the same winds blow, but less angrily, so that land and water, having struck a kind of truce, live in relative harmony.

The two kinds of coast meet at only one point, Cape Flattery, where the Pacific flows in and out of Puget Sound via the Strait of Juan de Fuca. When I was growing up in Washington, the cape was a place to be proud of and proprietary about, being not only the far northwest tip of our farthest-northwest state but also the closest point in the whole United States to the North Pole and the Orient. That particular pride of place now belongs to Alaskans, but Flattery is still a continental cornerstone, as wild a promontory as when Captain Cook sailed past it in 1778 without stopping and named it.

A year ago I revisited the cape—I suppose to satisfy myself that it was still there, still functioning as the boundary-marker between two kinds of coast. On a bright October morning I drove through the Makah Indian village at Neah Bay to the dead end of a rutted one-lane road. Somebody had put up a sign there: CAPE AREA TRAIL. RUGGED, HIGH CLIFFS. EXTREMELY DANGEROUS—ENTER AT OWN RISK. Along the trail the sword ferns were thick and almost shoulder high. The ground was muddy underfoot but the going was not bad because there were tangles of roots running out from big conifers that blocked the sky, and I could more or less step from root to root. After a while the scene opened up ahead through the cedars and spruces. I could see a number of little coves down below, boiling with surf. There was a loud roaring and hissing—the wind and the waves, both slamming in from the open Pacific—and as the water rose and fell, it kept filling and draining big caves that undercut the cliffs. Then I was at the end of the trail, standing 100 feet above the turmoil. My shadow stretched away out over the water toward Tatoosh, a flat-topped island with a lighthouse winking in its middle—on 24-hour duty to warn ships against the menacing rocks. Two gulls were suspended in midair between the cape and the island, flying into the wind with just enough energy to keep their speed over the water at zero. Right here, I thought, is where the irresistible force, 6,000 miles of ocean, meets the immovable object, 3,000 miles of continent—and they meet with one tremendous bang after another. Sound and fury and spray fill the air—air that is cleansing and bracing as it fills the lungs.

Geographically, Flattery will get you nowhere, for it is at the very end of the line. But it is a good place to stop, look and listen. So I stood for a while, just breathing and looking, trying to commit the whole spacious panorama to memory, knowing I might never return to this spot. The Washington shore stretched southward to my left in a long scallop of white beach, ending in a line of sentinel rocks at Point of Arches. Off to my right was the mouth of the Strait of Juan de Fuca, 15 miles wide, a roomy passage toward stiller waters for ships and seals and killer whales. On its far side lay the blue skyline of Vancouver Island's foothills, rising out of the unseen reefs that lie in wait to receive any ship that misses the strait, as some still do in fog and storm. Far beyond sight, about 100 miles off the coast, flowed the benign Japan

Unfurling along the curve of Rialto Beach in Olympic National Park, Pacific breakers churn up morsels for a flock of hungry gulls.

Current, the Pacific counterpart to the Atlantic's Gulf Stream. It is 75 miles wide and 300 fathoms deep, vaster than any landborne river, and by the time it has reached this point, far from its equatorial headwaters in the Philippine Sea, it has spent its force and is sluggish, moving only about a mile per hour. But its load of mild 50° water—65 million tons passing any given point every second—tempers the climate along the eastern rim of the Pacific for every form of marine and land life.

The current brings more than water across the sea. It bears glass fishing-net floats torn loose by storms off Japan and Soviet Asia, planks of teak and Philippine mahogany, long canes of bamboo and even an occasional derelict. Sometime back in the 1920s a Japanese fishing boat drifted ashore near Cape Flattery, with all hands long since dead of starvation. Their engine had broken down in a storm the year before, their gear was lost, and they had used up their strength trying to maneuver the ship back to the fishing banks. If they had spent their time luring fish, even straining plankton out of the water with their clothes, they might have lived, letting the inexorable current carry them where they ended up anyway.

A few misty miles south of Cape Flattery is Cape Alava, which reaches even a little farther into the ocean. One day, not long after my visit to Alava to inspect the site of the Makah Indian excavations there, I returned with a different purpose in mind: to hike a part of the Olympic National Park trail that begins at Alava and extends south for 50 miles. You need no guide in hiking it because the edge of the sea is itself the trail; nevertheless it is prudent to have a companion along. I had a particularly good one—David Huntzinger, whose official title is park staff interpreter. He is a naturalist for all seasons who has patrolled the coast even in the dead of winter, when the spindrift, the foam spun off the tops of angry seas, piles up knee-deep and rolls along the sand like white balls of tumbleweed.

We had barely started when Dave began to teach me some useful things to know while taking a wilderness-beach walk. For example, in exploring tidal pools, where both ground and water are carpeted with eelgrass, walk on grass that is brown, because it overlays solid rock; where the eelgrass is green there is water under it, and you can step in right up to your neck. In threading your way through fields of boulders that have eroded out of the cliffs, step only on rocks that are light colored, because that probably means they are dry. And step on their very tops, where your boots can claw in a little for better balance. Beware of the darker rocks, which may not be dry, and avoid rocks blotched with "tar spots," which are slippery as ice. The dark patches are *Ralfsia pacifica,* an alga covered with a slick, gluey surface that needs only occasional wetting by tide, rain or fog to keep the alga's cells growing. A misstep on *Ralfsia* can sprain an ankle or break a leg—one reason it is prudent not to be alone.

Dave also introduced me to his version of the trail lunch known as gorp: equal parts of raisins, peanuts, nonmelting chocolate candies, granola and bits of freeze-dried fruit, all tied in a plastic bag. There are as many recipes for gorp as there are hikers, and all provide fast energy: two handfuls will keep the stomach quiet for two hours. We were munching his particularly tasty gorp when we came to a hiker's choice. The short way around the base of a cliff led through a tumble of tar-spotted rocks. The long way crossed a fairly flat acre of tide pools. We took the long way in order to inspect the pools. The tide had just started to come in, and waves were roaring into some of the pools, drenching deep-blue clouds of mussels that covered the rocks. I am exceedingly fond of mussels but decided that this was not the time or place to gather them: there had been warnings of summer red tides that can cause paralytic shellfish poisoning.

On the undersides of rocks hanging over quieter pools, dozens of five-rayed starfish, some a bright orange and others an intense purple, clung by their multitudes of tube feet. We lifted up another kind of sucker foot, a 12-inch-long cryptochiton covered with eight leathery plates. It quickly contracted itself into the shape of a collapsed football, then expanded again when we returned it to its rock haven. At the bottom of one pool two hermit crabs, each about an inch long, played tag among small stones and conical limpet shells, while tugging along turquoise-colored snail shells that they were trying on for size. Nearby, three sea anemones the size of coffee cups gently waved their petal-like pink and green tentacles, and a couple of ugly-faced sculpins no longer than toothpicks cruised by, just out of reach. I fondled one of the anemones and let its stinging cells fondle my fingers; the tingling sensation was barely noticeable to me but would have been enough to anesthetize a small fish. The pools were crowded and busy, but we had to leave them, stepping carefully from one tan patch of eelgrass to another, before the tide cut us off.

The more you walk this coast the more you are impressed by the grand pattern on which it is constructed. The pattern is a procession of curving beaches, bold headlands and battered sea stacks, with unbroken forest looming along one driftwood-fringed flank and the never-silent sea encroaching on the other. The beaches are intermittently paved with black "rock sand" (ground-up basalt), off-white "shell sand" (ground-up shells and sandstone), pea gravel the consistency of slush, hand-sized stones patiently fitted into a mosaic by the waves and boulders waiting their turn to be hammered apart. Scattered on many beaches are pieces of sandstone and clay riddled with pencil-thick tubes. These holes are bored by the piddock clam, which drills rock as a shipworm drills wood, slowly rotating its body as it grinds out its burrow with the sharp edge of its shell. The piddocks are instruments of erosion, and sometimes a section of cliff that they assiduously honeycombed ages ago, before it was uplifted above tidewater, will break away and crash to the beach.

The headlands stand like high fortresses under siege by the sea. Some of them are unscalable and must be skirted at low tide, while others are unskirtable whatever the tide and must be scaled. The sea stacks are in various stages of erosion, some still attached to the land by sand spits, others cut off, some still bearing thatches of trees and some washed clean to the skeletal rock.

Every year more than 100 inches of rain falls on the coast, but the forest does its best to retard the runoff. In wintertime, freshets gush from every sopping bank; but in summer in most places there are only trickles and seeps dripping onto the beach. Most of them are drinkable and so are the few-and-far-between forest streams that cut shallow courses in the sand as they return to their source. Occasionally a 150-foot spruce or hemlock, its shallow root system undermined by one storm too many, topples majestically onto the shore to lie in state until another storm serves as its pallbearer, floating it off and then flinging it back on shore, perhaps miles away, to bleach among other driftwood.

A beach here is never empty. One day it may be strewn with long, bulb-ended whips of giant kelp, their holdfasts on the bottom torn loose by a storm. Next day the kelp will be gone but the sand may be littered with the feathers of moulting sea gulls, as if a pillow had been slit open. And every day on every tide, a cargo of intercontinental debris arrives on the beach: shoes and hatch covers, plastic bottles and Scotch bottles—enough of it to keep a park ranger busy. One evening I met a strapping young seasonal ranger, a college student named Mike Butler, who had earned a good night's rest at Cedar Creek after a hard day's stint working his way eight miles north from the coast town of La Push. His as-

Common to the Northwest coast, the shore birds at right all feed off the sea, but they exhibit distinctive tastes. The oyster catcher favors mussels as well as oysters, prying open the shells with its flattened bill; the western gull fares on dead fish, floating garbage and the young of other water birds. The pigeon guillemot prefers small fish like blennies, sticklebacks and sculpins, catching them near the surface, and the double-crested cormorant adds to this menu the larger herring, which it pursues by swimming underwater.

WESTERN GULLS

DOUBLE-CRESTED CORMORANTS

BLACK OYSTER CATCHERS

PIGEON GUILLEMOTS

signment was to pack whatever junk he could gather into plastic trash
bags so a helicopter could pick it up and cart it away. During the day,
he said, he had come across bear tracks among the footprints of gulls
and later, the black bear itself, getting a meal out of a dead porpoise at
the water's edge.

It is unusual to see land animals on the beach in daytime. Mostly
they are nocturnal visitors, and on any morning you may see signs that
skunks, raccoons, deer and even elk have ventured down to look for
food the night before, around the pools where the crabs and chitons,
starfish and anemones also feed. It is not unusual, though, to see more
eagles than people during the day. Not golden eagles, pantalooned with
feathers down to the feet, but American bald eagles, which go bare-
legged. Benjamin Franklin may have been right when he argued that
the useful turkey would have been a more appropriate national bird,
but the eagle is not entirely a good-for-nothing. It may be a lazy breed
of hawk, preferring to hijack fish from an osprey in midair to catching
its own, but it does police the shore and the riverbanks, helping to keep
them clear of carrion. It is somewhat misnamed, being not bald but
white-headed in maturity, and its purported prowess in carrying off
lambs and small children is distinctly exaggerated. Taking off into the
wind from water or level ground, it can lift half its own weight of 12 to
15 pounds, but with a plentiful diet of crippled sea birds, small fish,
squirrels, mice and shrews handy, it seldom needs to. (Its voice has
been exaggerated too—no strident scream, but only a thin yelp.) For all
its scavenging habits the bird is a great sight to see as it swoops down
from its lookout perch atop a tall cedar snag, seizes a poor fish in its talons with hardly a splash, then sails back into the trees with six-foot
wings pumping to gain altitude.

Eagles sometimes soar over Elephant Rock, a ponderous sea stack anchored squarely at the mouth of the Raft River, off the beach of the Quinault Indian Reservation 40 miles south of Cape Alava. The rock is 50
feet high, with a big hole in the middle. The sea rushes through and
bursts out the landward side like water sprayed from an elephant's
trunk. It makes quite a show, but fewer people see it these days because the Quinalt have closed their reservation beach to enable it to
recover from overuse by litterbugging tourists; it is off limits to any visitors not accompanied by a Quinault. My wife and I were there on a Sunday as guests of Guy McMinds of the tribal council. The Quinault
were having a picnic on the beach, the children playing a vigorous
game of softball. Their shouts could not compete with the noise of the

gulls. As we approached Elephant Rock, hundreds of these birds, raucous and busy, were fishing in the surf, joined by dozens of dusky cormorants. "Must be a lot of anchovies out there," Guy said, and as he spoke four big shapes glided through the crowd of gulls and cormorants. They were brown pelicans, far north of their California range and looking like a low-level flight of bombers. All four landed in the water at once and rested there, bobbing solemnly in the waves some distance from the gulls.

An even better place to see the birds of the Northwest coast at close range is Destruction Island, which lies four and a half miles offshore and about 25 miles northwest of Elephant Rock. Birds, in fact, are the only reason to go to Destruction Island; and the only way to go, unless you have your own boat, is to hitch a ride with the Coast Guard. Once a month a motor lifeboat sets out from the Coast Guard station at La Push (a corruption of the French *la bouche*), at the mouth of the Quillayute River. It makes the 30-mile round trip to check the diesel engines and the backup dry batteries that keep the Destruction Island automated lighthouse going. On the July morning I went out, there was a gentle rain and a slow ocean swell. We could see Mount Olympus for a few minutes, through a slit in the clouds, then lost sight of it for the rest of the day.

Years before, I had read about the bleak six-acre island in a W.P.A. Guide: "Nesting ground of some 10,000 horn-billed auklets, small migratory cousins of the great auk. Not unlike the penguin, they wear dress clothes of formal black or brownish black with a 'boiled front' of smoke gray, which extends down the flank. These birds . . . arrive during April and either use their old nest or dig into a hillside to make a new one. Their arrival is marked by a noisy shrieking."

Nowadays they are called rhinoceros auklets, after the small horn that develops on the beak in breeding season. We could just see them as Destruction Island became a low plateau on the horizon—perhaps 20 birds perched in a row on a drifting log. Instead of flying off like gulls at our approach, they hopped feet first into the water, where they taxied long distances, beating their stubby wings to get airborne. A wind might have helped, but there was none at the moment; some of the auklets just gave up and decided to dive rather than fly.

From the south side of the island we took a rubber dinghy into a cove where a steep cleated walkway leads up the bluff from a small concrete landing pier. As we climbed iron rungs set in the concrete, hundreds of western and glaucous-winged gulls, crowding every rock outcropping, greeted us with shrill cries of *ka-wee-ah, ka-wee-ah.* Two Coast Guardsmen were going to work at the lighthouse for a few days; they loaded boxes of groceries on a cart and I helped push it along rusted rails to a brick building that houses the diesels, the batteries and a bunkhouse. Salmonberry bushes have overgrown the rails and everything else on the island, and since they were dripping wet, so were we at the end of the 100-yard push. But I also had my fill of salmonberries, for the bushes were loaded.

A dead petrel lay in the grass outside the lighthouse door, and when I climbed the spiral staircase inside I saw the broken window the bird had crashed into. Attracted by the light, many passing petrels come to grief here every year. The lighthouse is on the seaward side of the island, and from the top I looked down on a series of rocky ridges that descend into the water. Each one was dotted with gulls, but no auklets were in sight; they were off for a day's fishing, not to return until evening. Later, however, I spotted a few of them as I pushed through a salmonberry thicket to get closer to the ridges. Several plump auklets, evidently getting a late start on their daily feeding foray, emerged from their burrows and took what seemed to be almost a running jump, plunging down to the water's edge in a maneuver apparently designed to gain flying speed.

Gulls and auklets can coexist on Destruction Island only because the latter go underground. Like most of the alcids, or diving birds—a family that includes the murres, the puffins and the pigeon guillemots—the auklets nest in tunnels that they dig as far as 20 feet into a steep bank, using their bills and their clawed, webbed, three-toed feet for earthmoving. It is at the terminus of the tunnel, which can be big enough for a man to crouch in if he could get there, that the female auklet's single white egg is laid and the chick is reared after it hatches, in about three weeks. Gulls would be happy to eat auklet eggs or chicks, but they never explore the dark burrows. They have a right to feel superior, however, when they see the awkward auklet come home from a fishing trip: it does not flutter gracefully to the ground but crash-lands in the brush, then picks itself up and lurches into its doorway. But in fishing technique the alcids have it all over the gulls. When they dive, sometimes to depths of as much as 100 feet, their foreshortened but strong wings enable them to fly through water, without use of the feet, and to catch up with any fish their superb underwater vision discloses. Small

Killer whales range the waters off the Washington coast in a menacing phalanx. When cruising in such packs, they are the sea's most treacherous hunters and are likely to take on any creature that swims, even 75-foot baleen whales three times their size.

herring and smelt sometimes make it simple for them, "balling up" into squirming masses that a bird, or a bigger fish, can gobble with ease.

Though nobody lives on Destruction Island, Gary Lentz, a pharmacy student at the University of Washington, once spent a month's leave there alone, when he served in the Coast Guard. Despite the lack of human company he was never bored for a minute, he told me. He saw harbor seals and sea otters sporting in the waters off the island, shrews scurrying in the brush at night, small salamanders at a fresh-water spring and a thriving sea-urchin population down in the tide pools. Along with auklets and gulls and petrels he spotted a pair of bald eagles and a number of crimson-beaked black oyster catchers.

"When you've got so many things to see," Gary said, "the time goes all too fast. I watched the gulls mating, then I would walk along the rocks and check their nests. I took several eggs to eat—only one out of a nest. They have a slightly fishy taste in the yolk, but if you scramble them with plenty of pepper they taste like other eggs. I can see why the Hoh Indians used to paddle all the way out to the island for clam and sea-gull-egg feasts." And I can see how Gary was sorry when his solitary month of leave was up.

There can be no question who is lord and master of the marine scene everywhere along this Northwest coast: it is *Orcinus orca*, the dread killer whale. The octopus and squid know it, the seals and fishes and birds know it, even the great blue, gray and sperm whales know it as an adversary as much to be feared as man, who is equally predaceous but less resourceful when it comes to killing. The high-pitched, clickity-clack "talk" of the killers carries for miles underwater, bearing a message of terror to anything that can hear or sense it. In the 1950s when white beluga whales were decimating the salmon run near the mouth of an Alaskan river, a Navy underwater-research team serenaded them with amplified tape recordings of killer-whale squeals and shrieks; the belugas got the message in no time and fled in panic out into the Bering Sea.

Fear of the killer whale is well grounded. It is the only marine mammal that preys on its fellow warm-blooded creatures (though not on its own species), as well as on cold-blooded animals. And no animal dares to prey on the killer. Charging at a speed of 30 miles per hour, it can overtake almost anything that swims and can swallow a seal as easily as a man downs an oyster. It can hunt in pairs or in well-coordinated packs of a dozen or more, circling and seizing sea lions or porpoises as

efficiently as wolves cutting caribou out of a herd. It is fearless in attacking a whale two or three times its size, slashing at the genitals, forc-
ing the mouth open to get at the tender tongue, finally feasting on the
disabled monster at leisure. Yet there is no proven record of a killer
whale intentionally attacking man, and every specimen that has ever
been taken into captivity, male or female, has actually seemed to enjoy human company.

Killer whales are at home in every ocean, but they find the waters of
the Northwest an ideal playground, probably because the cruising terrain, as well as the menu, is so variegated. From the rough open ocean
off Washington and British Columbia they can circle Vancouver Island
in either direction, using the Strait of Juan de Fuca and the Strait of
Georgia as two-way avenues to the shelter and the rich food supplies
of Puget Sound, the San Juan Islands and the Gulf Islands. In this inland sea they entertain the yachtsmen aboard one of the world's largest
concentrations of pleasure craft. Pods of killers are almost as familiar a
sight as boats, and their antics and acrobatics are exciting to watch.
They can fling themselves into the air with all the agility of leaping
tuna, and can even "walk on water" erect, balancing on their powerful,
wiggling tail flukes. Their showmanship may be one reason why they
go largely unchallenged by the "sportsmen" who use seals for target
practice. The killer whale's only commercial value is to aquariums, for
which a few are captured from time to time on order. As for enter-
tainment value, in or out of captivity, they are unmatched. The same
can be said for their brainpower, which—if their language is ever de-
ciphered—should make them of some scientific value as well. The
smartest Flipper-type dolphin or trained seal cannot compare to the killer whale in intelligence.

Like the dolphin, the porpoise, the sperm whale and the narwhal, the
killer is a member of the toothed suborder of cetaceans. The blue and
the gray whales, among other species, are in the whalebone or baleen
suborder; members of this branch of the family are toothless but have
intricate structures of whalebone in their mouths for straining food. No
whales chew their food, though the toothed whales may tear it into bite-
sized pieces; mostly they just bolt and gulp. Four dozen strong conical
teeth line the killer's capacious jaws, and its mouth holds a shell-pink
tongue the size of a platter.

Nobody can look on a killer whale and be unimpressed. For a ceta-
cean it does not grow to immense size, only 30 feet and 9 tons compared
to 100 feet and more than 150 tons for the blue whale, the largest an-

imal that has ever lived. It is in sheer beauty of coloration and configuration, and in its utter physical and intellectual mastery of its medium, that the killer is so impressive. From afar it can be identified by its high-rising dorsal fin, measuring up to six feet in the male, shorter in the female. Closer up, white patches over the eyes give the killer a masked-marvel look; its bottom and a saddle-shaped area behind the fin are also white on black.

Its flippers, protruding like hydrofoil fins, contain vestigial arm, wrist and finger bones, for the whale was once a land animal. Its sexual organs are retractable, for better streamlining. The single blowhole, which is atop the head, is a nostril that has evolved into an organ that controls breathing, and is used in communication (the killer whale has no vocal cords) and echolocation—the emission of clicks that bounce off objects near and far like sonar waves. It is probably a malfunction of the sense of echolocation that leads the whales to blunder up on a beach. Such stranding is fatal: deprived of the buoyancy of water, the whale's own weight collapses its lungs and it suffocates. Afloat in its own element it breathes air voluntarily, and in diving, with blowhole closed, it consciously restricts its blood circulation and oxygen supply to a minimum of vital parts—heart, brain, kidneys and the muscles needed for maneuvering. Killers probably dive no deeper than 300 feet and no longer than 30 minutes, though some of their big relatives go as far as half a mile down in order to catch and feed on the giant squid, the world's largest invertebrate.

There is some evidence that killers mate the year around. The 400-pound calf—one to a pregnancy—is born tail first and must surface immediately for its first breath of air. The mother has two nipples, one on either side of the genital area, and her calf nurses on her rich milk (35 per cent fat) for about a year while learning the skills of diving, hunting and echolocation.

I have met two pairs of killer whales, in British Columbia aquariums, and found all four of them playful, noisy and sexy. In each pair either the male or the female was not yet mature, but a great deal of amatory jostling and rubbing was going on between them. "Before long," I was told by John Colby, the young curator at Sealand in Victoria, "we may have an X-rated aquarium on our hands—and hopefully a whale calf." He bent over and gently brushed the sole of his shoe in the water, and almost at once a long pale shadow glided toward us from the other end of the open-air, million-gallon pool. At the exact point where John's foot had touched the water, a sleekly tapered head emerged. It was

Gingerly grasping a sea urchin it has picked off the Pacific floor, a sea otter surfaces to enjoy the snack. In its habitat among the rocks and kelp beds along the coast, the otter spends much time diving for food but more time floating comfortably on its back.

Chimo, a three-ton albino female, looking at us expectantly. I hesitantly patted the top of her glossy head, which felt like a wet football, and when she opened her mouth, I gingerly felt her pink tongue: it was like poking a thick piece of beefsteak. "Have a fish, Chimo," said John, dropping a small salmon into her gullet. Chimo snapped her jaws shut, submerged, sidled away and then happily hurled herself completely out of the water with an exuberant squeal, landing with a splash that deafened and drenched us.

Another fascinating marine creature of the Northwest coast, just as spectacular in its own way, is the octopus, to which silent movies gave a bad image it has never quite lived down. On screen, there was grim Hobart Bosworth in the murky ocean depths in his deep-sea diver's helmet and rubber suit, straining to free himself from a monstrous, slimy creature whose flailing tentacles kept coiling around him and his air hose in a horrid and possibly fatal embrace. The man-against-devilfish confrontation was inspired by a similar episode in Victor Hugo's *Toilers of the Sea,* but both were utter fakes. It is true that octopus outnumbers man eight arms to two; it is not true that an octopus would ever choose a human as a wrestling opponent, for in real life the creature is distinctly shy.

As in the case of the 10-armed squid, the nautilus and other cephalopods, life for the North Pacific octopus begins when sperm from the specialized copulative arm of the male fertilizes eggs within the mantle cavity of a female. (She can copulate only once in a lifetime, compared to three or four times a season for the male.) The sperm is implanted in a capsule in the female's body and may remain quiescent for weeks or even months, until she is ready for egg-laying. Once she deposits the eggs, up to half a million of them, in a crevice in some rocky underwater hillside, she spends the brief remainder of her life protecting them from small crabs, shrimp and various other predatory passersby until they can hatch.

Toward the end of a four- to seven-month brooding period the female eats nothing, and even fastidiously kicks away any stray floating bits of food lest they contaminate her eggs. By hatching time she has lost half her body weight, is within a week of death and has, in fact, started to decompose. But her work of carrying on the species is done. Her offspring, perhaps a quarter of a million larvae, free-swim in the water for a time; then the few that escape being eaten by predators settle down onto a sandy or pea-gravel bottom.

From the start the baby octopus is able to confuse an attacker, and perhaps disorient the opponent's sense of smell, by squirting sepia fluid from an ink sac located near the rectum. Another defense mechanism is a mottled surface of chromatophores, pigmented cells that the octopus can deliberately change in color and in texture and size as well, making it a better camouflage artist than the chameleon. It is an escape artist too, able to squeeze its arms and body through incredibly narrow spaces. Most important, it comes equipped with a brain and nervous system that are unmatched among invertebrates. Second only to such sophisticated mammalian thinkers as the dolphins and whales, the octopus is the smartest animal in the sea.

By the time it is a year old, weighing about a pound and with a one-foot armspread, it has found a nook or cranny to call home, perhaps in a rocky ledge below the waters of Puget Sound or the Strait of Juan de Fuca. A beak, parrot-like but upside down, has grown between the yearling's upper and lower jaws, strong enough to crack open a mussel or other thin-shelled mollusk. In another year, at five pounds and with three feet of tentacle spread, the octopus has built up a sizable garbage dump outside its hole, composed of discarded shell fragments and bones. By now it can move in like a torpedo on passing sculpins, perch and crabs, which it clutches, then paralyzes with its saliva and finally sucks clean. But one of the mainstays of its diet is clams. It thrusts one arm deep into the sand to grasp a clam, uses the jet stream of its siphon to wash the sand away and free the clam, then forces the shell open with two tentacles and severs the adductor muscle with its beak in order to gobble the clam on the half shell.

An octopus that lives out its five- to six-year life span may reach a weight of 100 pounds with a spread of eight feet. The biggest one ever measured in the Northwest was a 165-pounder taken at Sequim Bay, on the Strait of Juan de Fuca. Cecil Brosseau, director of the Point Defiance Aquarium, once encountered an even bigger one—aboard a boat in the Tacoma Narrows. The fishermen who caught it had already cut it up and stuffed it into sacks to take to market, but obligingly removed some of the remains so that Brosseau could have a look and take some measurements. He estimated that the octopus had a 24-foot spread and weighed 200 to 250 pounds. Such oversized specimens, Brosseau believes, are sterile but aggressive males that for some obscure reason are particularly gourmandizing eaters.

Everybody knows about the octopus' suckers, two rows of milky-pink suction cups that line the underside of each arm. Individually the cups are weak and easily pulled away from whatever they cling to, but collectively the thousand or so cups are so strong it may take a force of 500 pounds to pry a reluctant, fully grown octopus off a rock. The cups may continue to function for an hour or so after the creature's death; for that matter, the octopus can regenerate an entire arm after it is severed by an enemy. That also is well known; what was news to me was the fact that the octopus has not one heart but three, a systemic one and two brachial hearts located at the base of the gills for pumping blood into the arms.

To Brosseau, a self-taught marine biologist who has associated with octopuses since he was in his teens, the creatures display the rudiments of personality. At least there are strong differences in the behavior of the half-dozen specimens he keeps at the aquarium. Some simply eat their every-other-day herring and run, but one or two will linger to caress Brosseau with their arm tips for as long as an hour before getting bored and moving off.

"Not having a backbone to protect their nerve centers, octopuses don't like to be handled; they prefer to do the handling themselves," Brosseau told me. By way of evidence, he dipped a small herring into a tank, and a three-foot octopus instantly unglued itself from the opposite side and jetted across to grasp the fish. In a few moments the herring was handed from octopus arm to octopus mouth, was enveloped and vanished. One sinuous arm curled over the edge of the tank and around Brosseau's hand; the end of another arm went around my own wrist like a bracelet. "This is Mike," said Brosseau. "See, he responds to us by holding onto us." Mike's grip was gentle, not possessive. After a minute or so, he let go and swam away.

Just once, years ago, I traversed this coast by sea and saw how it must have looked to the Spanish and English explorers who beat their way north after rounding the Horn. The ship was the *H.F. Alexander,* in coastal service between California and Puget Sound; for her time she was a palatial, gleaming ocean liner, with all the amenities like shuffleboard and tea service on deck. I was 12 and my father had let me accompany him on a business trip, driving down the Pacific Highway from Seattle to Oakland. At San Francisco he put me aboard the *H.F.* on its northbound voyage, asked some friends to keep an eye on me, shook my hand and went off.

I think it was only the second day out when the ship's single-sheet newspaper reported that a great earthquake had shaken Japan. We were steaming north in a perfectly placid sea that afternoon when the western horizon lifted a bit and moments later, a towering wave struck us on the port side. We didn't capsize, like the fictional liner *Poseidon*, but the *H.F.* rolled like a cork before shaking off the blow. It was the tsunami, the giant tidal wave that is caused by undersea seismic convulsions, racing across the Pacific at hundreds of miles an hour, and it must have hit the beaches of Oregon and Washington like a seaborne avalanche. What damage it did there I do not know; we were too far offshore in the shipping lane to see.

But there were other excitements in store for a boy on his first sea voyage. Shortly before we rounded Cape Flattery to enter the Strait of Juan de Fuca I saw my first porpoises. A big school of them was cavorting a few hundred yards inshore from us and some were racing the ship, arcing in and out of the water in that graceful way in which porpoises half-swim, half-fly when moving at flank speed. I developed then and there an affection for the creatures that has never diminished.

Earl J. Larrison, a devoted biographer of the mammals of the state of Washington, seems to like the harbor porpoise as much as I do. Even its formal name, *Phocaena phocaena*, gives the creature a certain character: it comes from the French *porc-poisson*, literally pig-fish. "During the 10th Century," writes Larrison, "the meat of the porpoise was decreed, conveniently, by the Catholic church to be 'fish,' placing a price on the head of this whale. Transmuted, thus, to a fish, porpoise meat became a delicacy. King Henry VIII regarded 'polpess pudding,' a form of porpoise meat and sugar suspension, as his favorite Lenten dish. One early writer, however, says of the porpoise flesh that it is 'of a very hard digestion, naysome to the stomach, and of very grosse, excremental and naughty juyce.'"

To commercial fishermen the porpoise is naughty in general because of its omnivorous appetite for everything from crabs and eels to rock cod and salmon. Its favorite food, though, is krill, the tiny, shrimplike crustaceans that abound in colder North Pacific waters; it gulps them by the thousands.

Fortunately for the survival of the species, the porpoise has its own way of abounding. It breeds in late summer and early fall; the gestation period is about the same as for humans, and the female can mate immediately after giving birth. The young become fully grown in about 10 years—to about the same range of length and body weight as adult humans—and since they become sexually mature at the precocious age of

15 months, a cow can produce about 15 babies during her adult life-time. It is little wonder that next to the killer whale, the porpoise is the most abundant sea mammal along the Northwest coast. In recent years, however, their profligate growth has been somewhat hindered: Tuna fishermen have learned that hordes of yellow-finned tuna are often to be found feeding below schools of porpoises; no one has figured out why. Caught in the fishermen's nets, countless porpoises drown be-cause they cannot surface for air. The U.S. Navy may come to the res-cue of the species. Because of the creature's intelligence and amiable disposition, the Navy has found the porpoise eminently trainable for all sorts of undersea duty—potentially, perish the thought, even for laying and retrieving mines.

I thought of the porpoises and my first view of them from aboard the *H.F. Alexander* during my most recent look at the ocean coast. This time I was seeing it from a small plane. The pilot and I took off from the Makah Air Force Base—actually a radar station—near Cape Flat-tery. Below the starboard wing, the cape was taking its usual pounding from the waves. We headed south, past Cape Alava and along the state-ly procession of beaches, headlands and sea stacks. I clocked us as we flew over stretches I had hiked, and noted that distances that had taken a day to walk took minutes to cover by air. In 30 miles we saw no hous-es, no roads, no sign of life. But by then I knew something of the infinite variety of land and animal life that crowds every foot of land and water down there, and for the sake of all that life I hoped this would al-ways remain a wilderness coast.

A Brilliant Show at Low Tide

PHOTOGRAPHS BY ROBERT WATERMAN

The rhythmic tides that wash the Northwest coast also provide a fascinating bonus for watchers at the shore's edge: a twice-daily exhibit, in microcosm, of the life of the ocean floor. At many places along the coast when the tide goes out it exposes bare, rocky ledges pocked with cracks and depressions that remain partly filled with sea water. These natural aquariums, called tidal pools, harbor a startlingly beautiful profusion of sea-bottom plants and animals, fleetingly revealed by the tide's ceaseless cycle.

The basic flora of this open-air, undersea world are various types of algae, the green, red and brown seaweeds that provide nourishment and protection for the creatures of the pool. These plants often appear in bright, surprising colors.

Clinging firmly to the bottom and sides of the pools are crustaceans and mollusks, such as barnacles and mussels, that have no option to move when the tide goes out and that are adapted to endure brief periods of being high and dry.

In addition to these sedentary inhabitants, the pools harbor a mobile community of animals that find their way there or are stranded by low tide. These creatures, among them red and purple starfish, sea urchins, chitons and crabs, lead a somewhat unsettled existence at the sea's edge because on a rising tide the ocean surges over the rocks with great force, tumbling along with it everything that is not anchored down.

Turbulence is, in fact, a problem all sea-bottom plants and animals must cope with in an environment where the rule is hang on or die. They use a variety of devices and mechanisms. The limpet can anchor itself so firmly to rock that a man cannot dislodge it without breaking the shell; the sea anemone protects itself against turbulence—and from drying out when exposed—by folding its tentacles into its body and changing from a shimmering blossom to a motionless blob.

Other hazards besides the ocean's surge imperil the exposed communities: predatory birds find them easy pickings; evaporation of the shallow water increases salinity and decreases oxygen. Life in the pools goes on nonetheless, subject to rearrangement by each period of the tide. Soon after the close-up photographs on the following pages were taken, the pools were inundated, inevitably to reappear, but never again with precisely the same display.

Clusters of rock barnacles and blue mussels cling to the rock of a tidal pool —and to one another—amid a lush carpet of brown and green seaweeds. The dense seaweed cover, which provides shelter and sustenance for many of the animals, is the foundation of the tidal-pool community.

Its three-inch spines mostly out of water, a giant red urchin awaits the returning tide.

A blood starfish, so called for its color, reaches with one of its five arms to snare a snail.

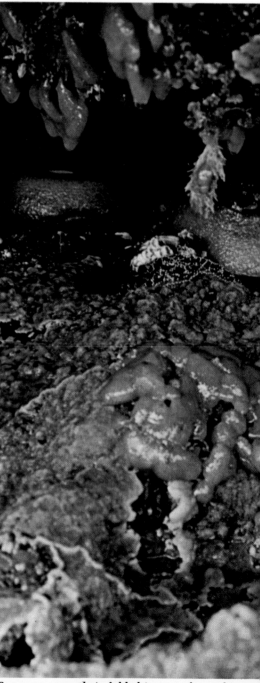

Sea anemones, their folded-in tentacles making

them look like baked apples, share a pool with bright pink algae, an upside-down starfish, mussels, barnacles and a giant chiton (foreground).

A hermit crab (above) emerges from the abandoned shell of a black turban snail; the claws of a smaller crab poke from a nearby shell. These soft-bellied creatures are named for their habit of tenanting empty shells, which they exchange for larger ones as they grow.

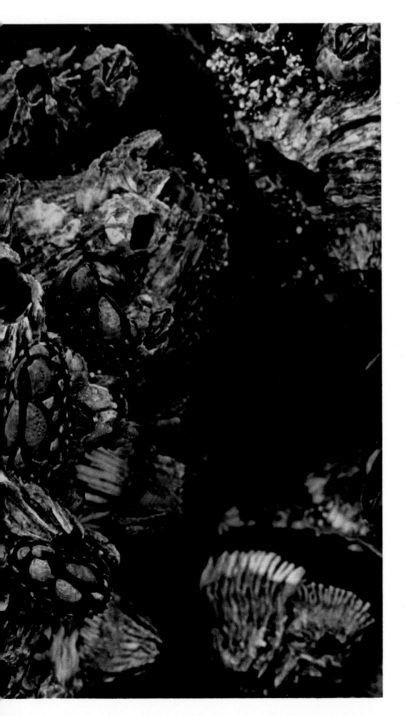

Crawling along the lip of a mussel, a young limpet searches for algae to eat. A limpet may spend all its life on one rock, making only short forays like this one when in need of a meal.

Rock barnacles cluster like miniature volcanoes on the shell of a large mussel, hedged around by smaller gooseneck barnacles. Permanently affixed by their heads, the barnacles, when submerged, use feathery feet to gather plankton from the sea water.

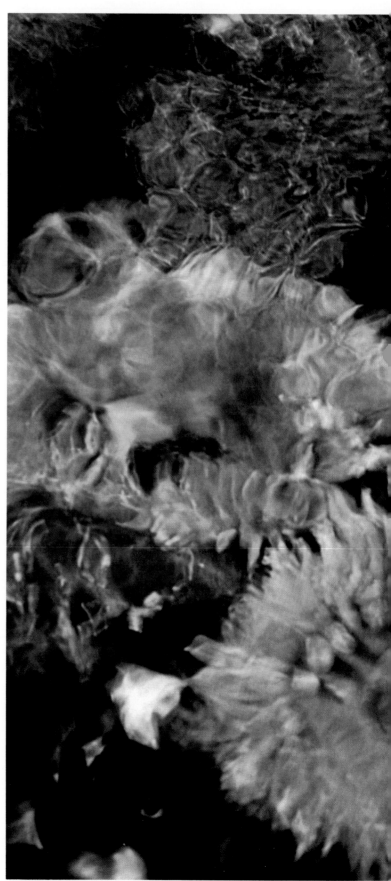

Strips of paper-thin green sea lettuce
set off an array of brown sea sac algae.
Seaweeds attach themselves to
objects by rootlike holdfasts, and
have a gelatinous coating that protects
them against the waves' friction.

Three green sea anemones shimmer
on the floor of a tidal pool that is
gradually being flooded by the
incoming tide. The creatures' color is
produced by chlorophyll-bearing algae
that live within their tissues.

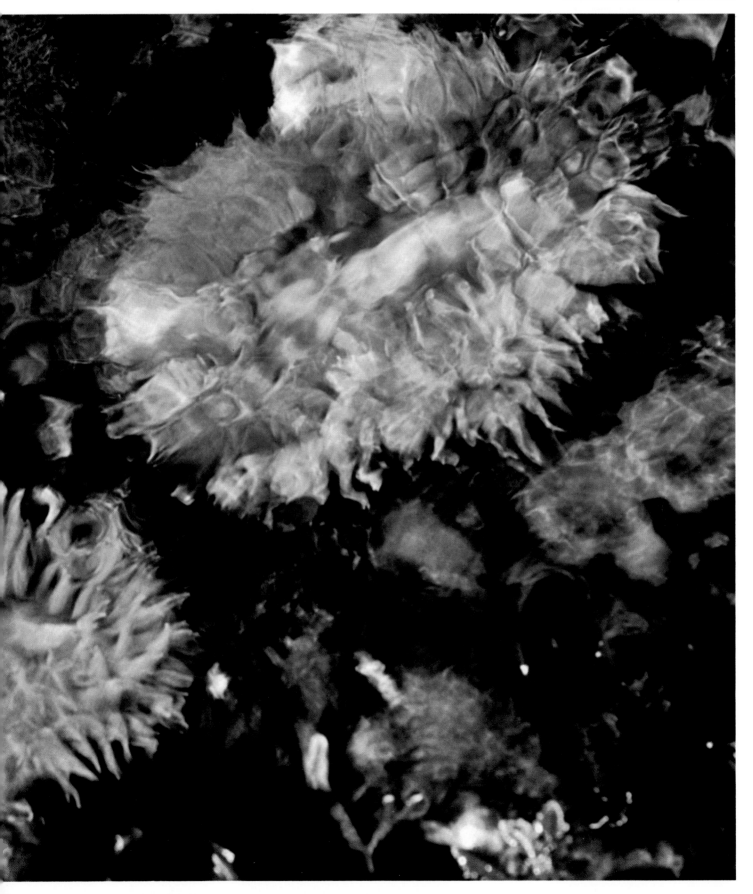

7/ From Kalmiopsis to Nitinat

---

*Like winds and sunsets, wild things were taken
for granted until progress began to do away with them.*

ALDO LEOPOLD/ *A SAND COUNTY ALMANAC*

The two of us were climbing a series of switchbacks in a trail that zigzagged up to the spine of a rocky ridge. My companion, a ranger named
Paul Brink, stopped, unshouldered his pack and bent down to tinker
with a black box wired to the trunk of a little pine tree.

"This counter is supposed to keep track of the traffic," he said. "Walk
through the light beam and we'll see if the thing clicks." The thing
clicked. "It says you are number 85 to pass this way this year. Of
course the counter can't discriminate between people and deer or bear
or cougar, so let's call it 85 large mammals. This isn't exactly what you
would call a crowded area."

We climbed a few hundred feet more up to the ridge crest and stopped
again for some deep breathing of the hot, dry air Far below and behind
us, west of the hazy blue coastal hills and about 20 miles away, the Pacific shore was shrouded in afternoon fog, suffused with bright gold by
the sun. Partly hidden by trees and not far ahead of us, but a good distance downhill, lay Vulcan Lake, where we would spend the night. We
were in the heart of the Siskiyou National Forest in southwest Oregon;
more specifically, we had just entered the Kalmiopsis Wilderness, a pre-
serve five times the size of Manhattan Island and a few million times
less populous—virtually uninhabited, in fact. The federal government
set this place aside in 1946, closing it to logging—and to all vehicles
—for the protection of such rare plants as the one the Kalmiopsis was

named for, a diminutive relative of the rhododendron. Wherever a back road touches the boundary of this wilderness now, a steel gate stops it from going farther.

Kalmiopsis: a name that is hard to get out of your head once it gets in. I had bypassed the place several times before I ever heard of it, but having once heard of it, I was hooked. There is something irresistible about a 100-square-mile area being called after a single, small unobtrusive shrub. The wilderness lies about halfway between the California line and the Rogue River, and is unlike any other along the Northwest coast; forested but not a rain forest, relatively arid in summer yet not a desert, a geological puzzle and a botanical marvel, supporting plants of ancient lineage that grow nowhere else. A lonely place, and a spooky one too: not far from here, early in World War II, a Japanese pilot flew in under cover of darkness to drop the only enemy bombs that ever fell on either United States coast, and made it safely back to the submarine from which he had been catapulted. He accomplished his mission, which was to start a forest fire, but Forest Service crews quickly got to it and put it out. Fragments of an incendiary bomb are still found occasionally near Wheeler Creek, and in 1962 the pilot, now middle-aged, was brought from Japan to be guest of honor at an azalea-festival parade in nearby Brookings, Oregon. He presented the town with his 400-year-old Samurai sword.

Nor is that the only curious story about this corner of the world. For years reports have come from the hills of repeated sightings of the Sasquatch, alias Bigfoot, a bigger-than-human counterpart of the Abominable Snowman of the Himalayas. He, or it, is alleged to skulk around remote ranches and mining cabins, and is said to have an appetite for raw meat that matches the cougar's. Years ago I was told of one rancher who used to put free meat out on a tree stump to feed a nine-foot-tall Bigfoot. The meat always disappeared, and then one night the rancher thought he glimpsed both a male and female Bigfoot, but he was unable to get a picture. It is probably just a tall story, though it is one I would like to believe.

So all those were reasons I wanted to see the Kalmiopsis for myself. Paul Brink, a summertime ranger from the state university at Corvallis, was the man to go there with: tall, wiry, full of youthful energy, he had hiked up and down this precipitous country many times. Now, after we had rested from our climb to the ridge crest, we crisscrossed our way down the far side, unslung our packs at the edge of Vulcan Lake and got down on all fours to dunk our faces in the water. It was cool but

In the hills of southwestern Oregon's Kalmiopsis Wilderness, sprigs of shrubby Sadler oak poke through the melting spring snow.

not cold, for the meltwater from winter snows had long since run off, and it was crystal clear. On the bottom, half a dozen of the black newts called water dogs, six or eight inches long, squiggled about on the hunt for food. Out in the middle, a few small trout were delicately nosing up to the surface, feeding on the evening hatch of flies and leaving delicate rings of ripples. Otherwise nothing riffled the lake or stirred the trees. On the opposite shore, where Vulcan Peak rose abruptly through 600 feet of jumbled yellow rockslide, the backdrop was a still life of great tawny stones and green trees, standing and fallen, with no call of a bird or crack of a twig to disturb the silence.

We clambered back over terraces of rock to unpack. All around us, poking out of every crevice, grew dark green, ground-hugging plants: the dwarf juniper; the matted squaw carpet, its bright blue flowers gone but its small branches seeking new chinks in which to root; the low-slung kinnikinnick and the canyon live oak, both creeping almost visibly in search not of light but of soil, in a terrain where crumbling rock abounds but soil is so scarce no grass can grow. The place was like a sprawling but carefully planned rock garden, and we stepped watchfully out of consideration for the struggling little shrubs. We smoothed away loose rock to make room for our sleeping bags, hung our packs high enough so they would not tempt prowling bears, ate our meal, swigged tin cups of tea and, in pitch-darkness, slipped into the sleeping bags. I wondered if any snakes would come to snuggle in with us for warmth, but need not have given that a thought: the air temperature was in the 80s and would stay there all night. Except for a brief crashing about in the brush a quarter mile away—a bear, perhaps, settling down for the night—everything was still. I lay for a long time staring up at the sky, thickly seeded with more stars than I had ever seen at once. It was the time of the Perseids, or shooting stars, and every few minutes a point of light would streak down and vanish, leaving only an after-image in the eye. I went to sleep thinking, with pleasure, that in all this 78,850-acre wilderness there probably were not a dozen other people spending the night.

In the morning Paul unfolded a map. "Before we walk out of here let's take a look at the lake down below this one. Its official name is Lish Lake, but I call it Little Vulcan. There are some interesting plants growing near it." We bushwhacked down through thickets of small pines and cedars and tangles of salal bushes and brown-barked manzanita bushes. Like its big brother, Little Vulcan Lake is an oasis in this arid, crackly wood, and along its marshy shore we came upon hundreds of Darlingtonia plants, glistening like so many graceful, golden-green cobras. The deadly simile is apt enough, for Darlingtonia is a meat-eating plant, like the Venus's-flytrap that captures and devours insects. Paul slit open the slender stalk of one of these beautiful carnivores. All the way down the viscous inside were the corpses of insects that had been lured to their death by Darlingtonia's sickly-sweet scent and were now in various stages of digestion.

On leaving the lakes we followed the traces of an old mining road strewn with fallen boulders, past the tailings and collapsed timbers of a chromium mine that had been worked during World War II, when even submarginal ores had been worth digging for the national stockpiles. Then the road petered out into a trail that edged along a sharp slope to emerge on a narrow hogback. On both sides of us, trees clung for dear life to steeply pitched cliffs. We sat on a rock there—it was like balancing on the edge of a knife—and after a while a bearded young man bearing a knapsack and a clipboard caught up with us. "I heard you, and thought I'd join you," he said. "I stepped on a little rattlesnake a few minutes ago. Didn't even see it until it went scooting off."

The Kalmiopsis is one of the more northerly parts of the rattlers' range but they abound there, evidently liking the heat and the dryness. They are shy, however, unless you somehow happen to corner them. Paul and I had seen no snakes, only a few lizards scuttling around the rocks. "What if it had bitten you?" I asked.

"We both have snake-bite kits," said Paul. "The best thing, though, is to be careful." With that laconic warning, he then introduced the newcomer as Norman Hamisch, a geologist from Palo Alto who was doing some mapping in the Kalmiopsis. "He's not the only one," Paul added. "This place is some kind of happy hunting grounds for geologists."

I remembered and quoted a phrase from Bates McKee's book *Cascadia,* which described the Klamath Mountains, including the Kalmiopsis, as "a genuine geologic nightmare," meaning that the record of the rocks in these hills is too confusing for a geologist's comfort. "So is this a nightmare or a paradise?" I asked Norman. He reflected a minute, then said with a grin that it was some of both. For one thing, most of the Klamaths are much older than other Northwest mountains; they were well into their fourth 100 million years before the Olympics were first thrust up from the sea. In that extra 400 million years the Klamaths have been subjected to that much more metamorphism under heat and pressure—so that their rocks have recrystallized into compositions

Two red buds of Kalmiopsis leachiana glisten in the May sunlight, on the verge of blossoming into small pink flowers. Ancient and rare, this low-growing relative of the rhododendron is found growing wild only in the region of the Kalmiopsis Wilderness.

whose origins are hard to trace—and to that much more weathering, folding and faulting.

Norman undertook to give me a brief lesson in rock identification. The crumbly, warm-colored rock that covered the hills was peridotite, an igneous rock; eons ago, when as lava it intruded into older rock, it had been a darker color, but had turned lighter, a kind of reddish tan, as it decomposed. Some of the peridotite had been transformed into a rock called serpentinite, all glossy and gray or green (it owes its name to its resemblance to snakeskin). The dark boulders we had seen along the old mining road were chromite, the stuff the miners used to dig out. "Geologically," Norman told me, "this area is in a critical condition; these mountains could be on the verge of sliding."

"You mean any minute now?"

"Well, not literally, but it's all very unstable stuff. You never know when a cliff is going to crack apart and tumble into a ravine." He stared out across the wilderness at the blotchily forested face of Pearsoll Peak, which lies just outside the Kalmiopsis boundary and at 5,098 feet is the dominant height in the area. It looked stable enough to me, though I thought the hogback on which we were perched was not very reassuring. "This is the weirdest place I've ever spent any time in," Norman said. "After a time it gives you an uneasy feeling that you'll never come to terms with it."

We got up and picked our way along the hogback. Off to one side, a thousand feet down, we could see a lake much smaller than Vulcan, looking as if the next rockslide would fill it up. On our left was an even deeper declivity; we could hear but not see the mountain stream that rushed along its bottom. Then we came to a little saddle hardly wider than a garden path, a small depression where moisture could gather and soil accumulate. Suddenly Paul stooped to examine the outcroppings of rock and the plants that grew around them.

It was in just such a place that the uniqueness of the plant that gave Kalmiopsis its name had been first recognized. In 1930 a botanist named Lilla Leach and her husband John, a Portland druggist, were hiking in these hills and came upon a patch of low evergreen bushes, covered with deep-pink flowers. After excitedly examining them, Mrs. Leach decided that she had never seen anything like this plant and that it must be new. She was right. Her find was not only new, in that it was previously undiscovered, but also incredibly old, dating back 150 million years to the time of the dinosaurs. Eventually the plant, so rare that it is in a botanical genus all by itself, was named both for Lilla Leach and for Peter Kalm, a celebrated Swedish botanist who had worked in America in the mid-18th Century and who had discovered certain plants related to the one Lilla Leach had found.

Paul suddenly found the little bushes he was looking for, and at last I gazed on *Kalmiopsis leachiana*. Healthy specimens, too, a foot to two feet across, huddled in low, graceful contours with hundreds of thick, glossy-green elliptical leaves the size of fingernails. Their bright blossoms had come and gone; all that was left to reward our two days' hike was a display of reddish-brown seed pods, peppercorn sized, some remaining on the shrubs and some scattered on the ground. I picked up a few seeds and held them in my palm; they were unremarkable, and certainly not as showy as the blossoms but I could not feel disappointed. Many a flower, after all, is born to bloom unseen, and not many people have the chance to see this plant, a survivor from the unimaginably distant past, in any of its seasons.

A couple of days later I had an eagle's-eye view of the whole Kalmiopsis Wilderness. In a Cessna 182, John Carter, the pilot, Don Wood, of the Forest Service, and I took off from Grants Pass and headed west across the rough canyons of the Rogue and Illinois rivers. We flew over Vulcan Peak and Vulcan Lake, skimmed the ridge where I had caught up with Kalmiopsis, and buzzed places with names like Babyfoot Lake and Tincup Creek. We saw hillsides carpeted with fir and pine, and even spotted a few droopy-tipped Brewer's, or weeping, spruce, one of the world's rarest conifers. Some of the slopes that had seemed so arid on the ground looked like soft, green, brushed velvet from the air, with silvery snags rising out of them like toothpicks.

"Old burns," said Don Wood. "Some were lightning fires, some were set by Indians to drive game into a pocket." We cruised past the fire lookout shack on top of Pearsoll Peak and I waved, in case the ranger on duty was looking up at us. His stilted station was the only sign of human presence for miles around, and I found myself envying him. For a long, therapeutic dose of solitude, with almost no other human beings to be encountered in all the vast and silent landscape, the Kalmiopsis would be my choice.

In a very different kind of wilderness, 600 miles north by west from the Kalmiopsis across the states of Oregon and Washington and the Canadian border, is the most spectacular single sight in the whole Northwest coast. A river, streaming out of a lake on Vancouver Island, glides past giant cedars to its rendezvous with the sea—and plunges right over a broad cliff to dash itself 60 feet below on the Pacific Ocean beach. It is as though the entire island had just sprung a gigantic leak. I have never seen anything like it.

Few people, in fact, ever do get to see Tsusiat Falls, or to swim in the lovely pool the torrent has scooped out at its base, where the sound of cascading fresh water sometimes drowns out the drumming of the surf. It is not an easy place to reach. The approach by land requires a strenuous walk through difficult forest terrain, and the approach by sea is worse—rocky, often wave-slashed and altogether risky. Indeed, for some doomed souls, clinging to the spars of ships that were being dashed ashore in storms, the awesome water curtain of Tsusiat Falls, looming beyond the foaming, terrifying breakers, has been the last thing their eyes beheld.

Though they differ vastly in looks, Tsusiat Falls and the Kalmiopsis have a bond. Each is, in its own way, a last redoubt of a dwindling wilderness. Some of the Oregon shoreline has been transformed into a gaudy ribbon of seaside resorts; some of the Vancouver Island coast has been logged, and has taken on a settled look, and some is becoming a recreation area. But just as civilization is a long way away high in the dry Kalmiopsis hills, so too, for a 57-mile stretch along the weather-beaten southwestern edge of Vancouver Island, the coast is still wonderfully untamed. Tsusiat Falls thunders onto the rocky beach in just about the middle of that rugged strip.

Four miles down the coast from the falls is Nitinat Lake, a tidewater lake 15 miles long and a mile and a quarter wide, whose outlet to the ocean narrows to 80 feet to become a raging impassable millrace with every advance and retreat of the tide. Only during periods of slack current at low tide is it safe to cross this channel; people have drowned trying to swim it when the sea was rushing in or out.

It is said that in the days when the Nitinat Indians lived in this land the salmon used to crowd so thickly through the entrance from the sea into the lake that one could almost walk across on their backs. This bounty made Nitinat Lake an invaluable resource to the Indians, and they sometimes barricaded the turbulent narrows with driftwood log fortifications to keep their enemies from the salmon. (Except for an unusual run in 1972, the area has now been largely fished out for salmon, but other kinds of fish, and often crabs too, still sluice back and forth from lake to sea.)

The Nitinat, a subtribe of the Nootka Indians, were superb wood carvers, whose cedar-log canoes were among the finest made. Their source of supply was one of the purest stands of western red cedar anywhere along the coast, and their exquisitely carved, eminently seaworthy canoes were bartered at good profit to their parent tribe up at Nootka Sound and to their cousins the Makah, down on the other side of Juan de Fuca Strait.

Along with their boatbuilding skills, the Nitinat were also master carvers of the great tall totem poles that the Indians in this part of the world erected to stand as heraldic symbols before their houses and as sentries before their villages. Sometimes, when I have come upon the grotesque whitened skeletons of lightning-struck cedars that stand here and there in the coastal forest, I have wondered whether it was not such ghostly spars, into which it is easy to read the deformed features of men and beasts, that first inspired the Indians to execute their goblinesque masterpieces.

Connecting Lake Nitinat and Tsusiat Falls, and extending beyond them for a total distance of 57 miles, is the West Coast Life-Saving Trail. It is a man-made trail that does little or no violence to the wilderness area around it, though paradoxically it was built to make that wilderness more accessible. This remarkable project had its roots in the number of shipwrecks that occurred along the Vancouver Island coast. Captain James Cook negotiated the coast and made it without mishap in and out of rock-bound Nootka Sound, the Indians' main stronghold, in 1778. But Cook was a superb navigator, and later seafarers were less fortunate. In the late 19th Century dozens of ships bigger than Cook's, heading for the Strait of Juan de Fuca, piled up instead on the reefs to the north. Hundreds of lives were lost in the hammering surf, but even survivors had a perilous time of it. A sailor who managed to struggle safely to shore was likely to die of exposure before he found his way to civilization.

To give survivors an escape route, the Canadian government in 1890 began building a trail leading southeast to northwest, from the logging town of Port Renfrew to the fishing village of Bamfield, and a telegraph line was strung from tree to tree along the route between the two hamlets; the linemen who patrolled and maintained it served as lifesavers on the side. A wrecked mariner who succeeded in struggling to shore would now at least have a fighting chance. He would find the telegraph line, if he still had the strength, and follow it.

Then in January 1906 the steamer *Valencia*, two days out of San Fran-

On the wild western rim of Vancouver Island, a graceful conifer loops over Little Tsusiat Lake, cluttered with driftwood piled up by the current. The lake drains its bigger neighbor, Tsusiat Lake, and itself flows into the mile-long Tsusiat River, which in turn plunges directly over a waterfall onto a Pacific beach (pages 170-171).

cisco, smashed ashore in thick weather near Pachena Point, eight miles
northwest of Tsusiat Falls. Of 164 passengers and crew, only 38 survived the wreck. Many years later, Bruce Scott, an Australian who
spent three decades at the Bamfield cable station, wrote a footnote to
the *Valencia* tragedy in *"Breakers Ahead"*:

"The following summer, while exploring a cave 200 yards from the
wreck, Indians in a dugout canoe discovered one of the *Valencia*'s life-
boats containing eight skeletons lodged inside. The cave . . . was a large
one 50 feet high and 200 feet long with a large boulder blocking the entrance. The lifeboat must have been lifted bodily over this rock at high
tide and, once inside, [the passengers] could not escape. It was a per-
fect man trap."

The mass disaster led the Canadian government to improve what became known as the Life-Saving Trail. Twenty-one suspension bridges
were thrown across streams, aerial cars or boatswain's chairs were
hung on wires across rivers, and shelters equipped with telephones
were erected every six miles. There have been many more shipwrecks
since then, and the trail has saved many lives. But new navigational
aids have made the coast somewhat less of a nemesis to shipping, and
air-sea rescue techniques have been developed over the years; today
the trail is a hiker's delight, and so is the area around it.

Still wilderness, all but roadless and with a population density of
near zero, it is one of the few areas on Vancouver Island that have not
been logged, converted to farming, or bought up for other development. One particularly enchanting stretch is that part of the hinterland
known as the Nitinat Triangle, a pie-slice of virgin country nestled between two heavily timbered ridges. The 13,200 acres of the triangle enclose a cluster of four beautiful lakes—Hobiton, Tsusiat, Squalicum,
Tsuquadra—and provide a haven for remnants of deer, bear and cougar populations, plus even a few representatives of the nearly extinct
Vancouver Island wolf, an elusive gray ghost wilder than anything else
in the dog family.

Whether the triangle will remain pristine is another matter. For some
years an argument has surged over the question of how much of this
area of lovely lakes should be preserved as wilderness and how much
should be logged or developed. Canada's Pacific Rim National Park, created in 1971, included from its beginning the Life-Saving Trail itself, as
well as miles of splendid sandy beaches and island groups that lie farther up the Vancouver Island coast. But the original protected area

where the trail runs included only a half-mile-deep strip along the shore. Up to that narrow green belt loggers were allowed to clear-cut to their hearts' content. In 1969 conservationists mounted a campaign to save the shore strip from the saw. They sought to have it made at least a mile and a half deep so the forest would have enough depth to protect itself against the storms that ravage it every winter. They also urged that the Nitinat Triangle, with its animals and its precious stand of primeval trees, be included.

The controversy will probably never be solved to everyone's satisfaction, but in 1972 the conservationists scored a major triumph when the provincial government of British Columbia banned further logging in the triangle.

No laws are permanent, of course, but chances are that this coastal wilderness will survive. To see it is to know why it should be saved. Strewn with battered hulks and rusting anchors, the desolate shore is one of the most beautiful pieces of ocean-front real estate in North America. Like the rest of the Pacific shore from the Aleutians down to California, it is studded with steep headlands, but with much larger crescent beaches scalloped between them.

Massed in back of the shore are magnificent stands of western red cedar, Sitka spruce and western hemlock, some of the trees eight feet thick and more than a thousand years old. In dark damp places the forest floor is covered with the inelegantly scented skunk cabbage, which in springtime erupts in great bursts of yellow flowers among its two-foot jade-green leaves. Where the trees' canopy admits more sunlight, prickly-leaved salal bushes grow eight feet tall, in nearly impenetrable thickets that provide the sweet-and-sour salal berries that the bear and deer love. Cutting through these forests, the unfordable but raftable Gordon and Klanawa rivers spill out to tidewater along with more than 30 other streams, including the Tsusiat. At the sea's edge are long straightaways where shelving sandstone forms a broad, smooth sidewalk at low tide. This natural pavement is broken here and there with chasms cut by the sea, as abrupt as the cracks opened by earthquakes. It is also puddled with tidal pools that are crowded with sea anemones, chitons and crabs.

Life, in fact, teems on the shore. Not far off Pachena Point, for instance, the gulls and other shore birds share a wave-swept rock with a noisy rookery of northern sea lions. These are among the loudest of sea mammals, and their braying bellow carries on the wind for miles across the water. The male grows to 12 feet in length and more than a ton in weight, which makes him much larger than the California species, and with only the killer whale to fear among ocean creatures, he is lord of these coastal waters.

Flopping around on a rock, the sea lion is a clumsy beast; in the water it is a swift and graceful swimmer, moving with a sinuous, undulating style that has led more imaginative observers to mistake it for a sea serpent. Unfortunately some people have also mistaken it for an enemy. Until a few years ago there was actually a price on its head: the Canadian government paid a bounty to killers of sea lions, as well as of the much smaller hair seals and harbor seals, because these creatures made depredations (actually inconsequential) among salmon, halibut and other commercial fish. The sea lions were all but exterminated before they were tardily granted legal protection; but passing fishermen with rifles in their boats still take pot-shots at both sea lions and seals —sitting ducks on their exposed rocks—just for the sport of it and perhaps out of some sense of mission: the fewer predators of fish, the more fish for the fishermen.

So, although sea lions can be viewed in their natural habitat on the rocks off Pachena Point, they are understandably gun shy. The only one to whom I ever got close enough to meet personally was a domineering, 400-pound yearling bull named Sam, in the Vancouver aquarium. He stopped bullying a little brown cow long enough to come over and let me feel his wiry whiskers and stroke one tiny ear, then uttered a derisive and deafening bark, half bellow and half belch, and plopped back into his tank.

The sounds of the sea and of the sea lions along the Vancouver coast are augmented by the never-ceasing cries of its sea birds—essentially the same as those that live on the Washington and Oregon coast. One species that I found as interesting as the rhinoceros auklet of Destruction Island was the marbled murrelet, a small, thick-necked bird that mingles on the water surface with the gulls and puffins. Its summer plumage is dark brown, flecked or marbled with white; in wintertime it is white from the "waterline" down and slate gray on top.

Every evening during the breeding season, after feeding on small fish and crustaceans, all the marbled murrelets in an area circle skyward in a flock, as if on signal, to gain altitude and then speed inland—destination unknown. No one knows whether the nests to which they carry food for their young are in trees or in cliffs; no nest has ever been positively identified. Nor has anyone, ornithologist or layman, ever laid eyes on the bird's newly hatched downy young, though a few brown speckled eggs have been found on the ground under trees. The young that have been reared at the nesting sites appear offshore at the end of June, half a dozen or more being chaperoned by two or three 10-inch-long adults. But where they all go to spend the night has long been an intriguing mystery.

The mystery will be solved one day, but that will not detract from the pleasure of walking the Life-Saving Trail. It offers so much else to enjoy as it meanders through groves of immense cedars, spruces and hemlocks, or skirts a mile-long curve of gray sand—always within sound of the ocean waves, but seldom within sight of them. Of course, the trail also has its hazards, and they are not to be ignored. It is roller-coaster steep in places, and though there are bridges over the Tsusiat and a few other rivers, the suspension spans over some streams have rotted away. Dozens of deadfalls block the way, slick logs that demand high-wire-walking skill are the only way across many streams and there are spots where you must either have a canoe, build a raft or hope a friendly Indian will come and ferry you over an unfordable waterway. Furthermore, it rains a lot.

Nevertheless at least 2,000 serious hikers a year make the week-long journey from one end of the trail to the other. None of them is ever likely to forget it, for—like a climb past Blue Glacier, a walk into the Kalmiopsis or a pack trip through the Bogachiel rain forest—the trek along the Life-Saving Trail is a wilderness experience that is not simply handed to you but pounded into you at every step, to stay in your bones, your muscles and your memories forever.

Along the Life-Saving Trail

PHOTOGRAPHS BY STEVEN C. WILSON

Most wilderness regions have one dominating and distinctive aspect. But along the southwestern coast of Canada's Vancouver Island, where dense forest and open ocean meet, both land and sea assert their own claims, offering an assortment of impressions and contrasts.

For photographer Steve Wilson, who took the pictures that follow, the contrasts began at the very shoreline. At the forest's edge frail wild flowers nestled in massive cliffs, while the waves below, deceptively softened by fog, smashed violently against the rock foundations. Wilson recalls that it took but a moment to pass from the noise and restlessness of the ocean into the silence of the woods. Here he saw leafless trees like transfixed specters. They had died centuries ago, yet they still stood—preserved, almost pickled, by the wet, salty air.

In this harsh, seemingly inhospitable place Wilson found another contradiction—a surprisingly comfortable environment in which he sustained himself for 10 days. For lodging, he occupied a large dry cave on the beach not far from Tsusiat Falls, on the 57-mile West Coast Life-Saving Trail. To supplement his own rations, he had only to stoop here and there along his favorite part of the trail, the seven miles between the Klanawha and Cheewhat rivers. Ingredients for his evening meals included mussels, clams, wild onions and parsley; one day he even found a bottle of sake that had washed ashore from a Japanese ship.

In his explorations Wilson became increasingly aware of the diversity of shapes around him. On the beach, viewing the ocean's immense expanse, he noticed the horizon delineating the earth's curvature, a shape his camera emphasized in the pictures on pages 168 and 169. Contained within this terrestrial curve were smaller shapes that blended or clashed or even duplicated one another. As he explains it: "A wave, after it has broken, has a disturbed, mottled surface. Sandstone eroded by the waves seems to reproduce this surface; it looks as fluid as the ocean." The details of the forest —the shape of a dead branch or the eerie formation of moss seen close up—also absorbed Wilson, so much so that one night, as he was returning to camp, he realized he had traveled no more than 100 yards that day. "I thought I was miles away," he says. "It took me just two minutes to get back to my cave."

SANDSTONE LEDGES ERODED BY WAVE ACTION

A STAND OF SPRUCE NEAR NITINAT NARROWS

CLIFF-HANGERS: INDIAN PAINTBRUSH, WHITE STRAWBERRY BLOSSOMS, BLUE-EYED GRASS

TSUSIAT FALLS: A 60-FOOT PLUNGE INTO THE PACIFIC

WAVE-CARVED ROCKS NORTH OF NITINAT NARROWS

A TWO-MOUTHED CAVE NEAR TSUSIAT FALLS

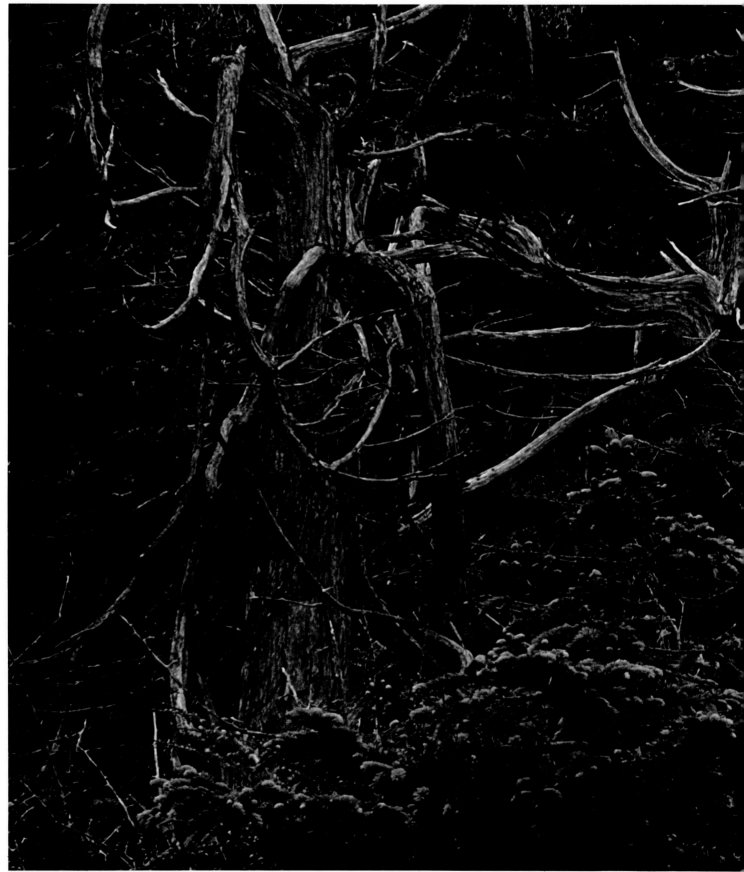

DEAD TREES IN THE COASTAL FOREST

ROCKS UNDER THE OCEAN'S ASSAULT

MOONLIGHT ON A MAGNIFIED WISP OF MOSS

WIND-STUNTED SPRUCE TEETERING ON A CLIFFSIDE

11111

Bibliography

*Also available in paperback.
†Available only in paperback.

Amos, William H., *The Infinite River*. Random House, 1970.

Andrews, Ralph W., *Curtis' Western Indians*. Superior Publishing Company, 1962.

Angell, Tony, *Birds of Prey on the Pacific Northwest Slope*. Pacific Search, 1972.

†Arnold, Augusta Foote, *Sea-Beach at Ebb-Tide*. Dover, 1968.

Baldwin, Ewart M., *Geology of Oregon*. University of Oregon, 1964.

Bartsch, Paul, and John T. Nichols, *Fishes and Shells of the Pacific World*. The Macmillan Company, 1945.

Bascom, Willard, *Waves and Beaches: The Dynamics of the Ocean Surface*. Anchor Books, 1964.

Berry, James Berthold, *Western Forest Trees*. Dover, 1966.

†Brown, Vinson, and Ernest Braun, *Exploring Pacific Coast Tide Pools*. Naturegraph Company, 1966.

†Carl, G. Clifford, *Guide to Marine Life of British Columbia*. British Columbia Provincial Museum, 1971.

Colson, Elizabeth, *The Makah Indians*. University of Minnesota Press and Manchester University Press, 1953.

Dalquest, Walter W., *Mammals of Washington*. University of Kansas, 1948.

†Danner, Wilbert R., *Geology of Olympic National Park*. University of Washington Press and Olympic Natural History Association, 1970.

*Douglas, William O., *My Wilderness: The Pacific West*. Doubleday & Company, 1960.

†Drucker, Philip, *Indians of the Northwest Coast*. The Natural History Press, 1955.

†Fagerlund, Gunnar O., *Olympic National Park, Washington*. Government Printing Office, 1965.

†Friedman, Ralph, *Oregon for the Curious*. Pars Publishing Company, 1972.

Haskin, Leslie L., *Wild Flowers of the Pacific Coast*. Binfords & Mort, 1967.

Hitchcock, C. Leo, and Arthur Cronquist, *Flora of the Pacific Northwest*. University of Washington Press, 1973.

Hult, Ruby El, *The Untamed Olympics*. Binfords & Mort, 1954.

Ingles, Lloyd G., *Mammals of the Pacific States*. Stanford University Press, 1965.

Jewitt, John R., *Narrative of the Adventures and Sufferings of John R. Jewitt*. Ye Galleon Press, 1967.

*Johnson, Myrtle Elizabeth, and Harry James Snook, *Seashore Animals of the Pacific Coast*. Dover, 1967.

Kirk, Ruth, *Exploring the Olympic Peninsula*. University of Washington Press and Olympic Natural History Association, 1969.

†Kirk, Ruth, *The Olympic Seashore*. Olympic Natural History Association, 1962.

Kirk, Ruth, and Johsel Namkung, *The Olympic Rain Forest*. University of Washington Press, 1966.

†Krenmayr, Janice, and Bob and Ira Spring, *Footloose around Puget Sound*. The Mountaineers, 1970.

†Larrison, Earl J., *Washington Mammals: Their Habits, Identification, and Distribution*. The Seattle Audubon Society, 1970.

†Larrison, Earl J., and Klaus G. Sonnenberg, *Washington Birds: Their Location and Identification*. The Seattle Audubon Society, 1968.

Lee, W. Storrs, ed., *Washington State: A Literary Chronicle*. Funk and Wagnalls, 1969.

†Leissler, Frederick, *Roads and Trails of Olympic National Park*. University of Washington Press, 1971.

McKee, Bates, *Cascadia: The Geologic Evolution of the Pacific Northwest*. McGraw-Hill, Inc., 1972.

Morgan, Murray, *The Northwest Corner: The Pacific Northwest, Its Past and Present*. The Viking Press, Inc., 1962.

Peattie, Roderick, ed., *The Pacific Coast Ranges*. The Vanguard Press, 1946.

Post, Austin, and Edward R. LaChapelle, *Glacier Ice*. The Mountaineers and University of Washington Press, 1971.

†Rice, Tom, *Marine Shells of the Pacific Northwest*. Ellison Industries, Inc., 1971.

Ricketts, Edward F., and Jack Calvin, *Between Pacific Tides*. Stanford University Press, 1968.

Scheffer, Victor B., *The Year of the Seal*. Penguin Books Ltd., 1973.

†Seed, Alice, ed., *Sea Otters in Eastern North Pacific Waters*. Pacific Search, 1972.

†Seed, Alice, ed., *Seals, Sea Lions, Walruses*. Pacific Search, 1972.

†Seed, Alice, ed., *Toothed Whales in Eastern North Pacific and Arctic Waters*. Pacific Search, 1971.

Smith, Lynwood, *Common Seashore Life of the Pacific Northwest*. Naturegraph Company, 1962.

†Stewart, Charles, *Wildflowers of the Olympics*. Nature Education Enterprises, 1972.

Swan, James G., *Almost Out of the World*. Washington State Historical Society, 1971.

†Wilhelm, Eugene J., Jr., *Common Birds of Olympic National Park*. Olympic Natural History Association, 1961.

Wood, Robert L., *Across the Olympic Mountains: The Press Expedition, 1889-90*. The Mountaineers and University of Washington Press, 1967.

Wood, Robert L., *Trail Country: Olympic National Park*. The Mountaineers, 1968.

†Yocom, Charles, and Raymond Dasmann, *The Pacific Coastal Wildlife Region*. Naturegraph Company, 1965.

Acknowledgments

The author and editors of this book are particularly indebted to Victor B. Scheffer, Chairman, The Marine Mammal Commission, Bellevue, Washington; and Richard W. Fonda, Associate Professor of Biology, Western Washington State College, Bellingham, Washington. They also wish to thank the following persons and institutions in Washington—At Olympic National Park, Port Angeles: Roger Allin, Superintendent; Reed Jarvis, Assistant Superintendent; Craig Blencowe; Robert Cates; Bruce Collins; Lloyd Dickerson; William Ferraro; David H. Huntzinger; Robert W. Kaune; William Lester; Bruce B. Moorhead; David Reaume. With the Quinault Resources Development Project, Quinault Tribal Council, Taholah: Guy McMinds, Director, Brian Allee and John Bryson. With the U.S. Coast Guard, Neah Bay: M. L. Campbell, Chief Warrant Officer; John L. Case, Chief Engineer; Gregory J. Swaney Sr., Officer in Charge, Cape Flattery. At the University of Washington, Seattle: Kenneth Chew, Professor of Fisheries; Lauren Donaldson, Professor Emeritus of Fisheries; Alyn Duxbury, Research Associate Professor, Department of Oceanography; Edward R. LaChapelle, Associate Professor of Geophysics; Vance Lipovsky, College of Fisheries; Robert T. Paine, Professor of Zoology; Sigurd Olsen, Affiliate Assistant Professor of Fisheries; Grant Sharpe, Professor of Outdoor Recreation, College of Forest Resources; Daniel Stuntz, Professor of Botany. And also: Ernest Brannon, Dungeness Hatchery, Department of Fisheries; Cecil Brosseau, Director, Point Defiance Public Aquarium, Tacoma; Richard D. Daugherty, Professor of Anthropology, Washington State University, Pullman; Carl English, Seattle; Gunnar O. Fagerlund, Sequim; Glen Gallison, National Park Service, Pacific Northwest Region, Seattle; Harry Majors, Seattle; Harvey Manning, Issaquah; Mark Meier, U.S. Geological Survey, Water Resources, Tacoma. In Oregon—Paul Brink, Chetco Ranger Station, Brookings; Jerry F. Franklin, Principal Plant Ecologist, U.S. Department of Agriculture, Forestry Sciences Laboratory, Corvallis; Carl E. Gohs, Portland; Dr. and Mrs. Edward Winslow Harvey, Astoria; William P. Ronayne, Superintendent, and Don Wood, Siskiyou National Forest, Grants Pass. In British Columbia, Canada—At Sealand of the Pacific Ltd., Victoria: John Colby, Curator; R. H. Waters, Administrative Manager, and R. H. Wright, President. Also: R. Wayne Campbell, British Columbia Provincial Museum, Victoria; Rick Careless and Rod Gee, Sierra Club of British Columbia, Victoria; Gil Hewlett, Curator, Vancouver Aquarium; R. Bruce Scott, Victoria; John Willow, Victoria. And also—Brock Evans, Sierra Club, Washington, D.C.; Sidney S. Horenstein, Department of Invertebrate Paleontology, The American Museum of Natural History, New York City; H. Douglas Kemper, Associate Curator, New York Aquarium, New York City; Larry G. Pardue, New York Botanical Garden, New York City; Dixy Lee Ray, Chairman, U.S. Atomic Energy Commission, Washington, D.C.; Parke Snavely and Rowland W. Tabor, U.S. Geological Survey, Menlo Park, California.

Picture Credits

The sources for the pictures in this book are shown below. Credits for the pictures from left to right are separated by semicolons, from top to bottom by dashes.

Cover—Harald Sund. Front end papers 2, 3—Harald Sund. Front end paper 4, page 1—Harvey Lloyd. 2, 3—Harald Sund. 4 through 7—Jim Brandenburg. 8 through 13—Harald Sund. 18, 19—Maps by Hunting Surveys Limited. 22—D. C. Lowe. 26, 27—Harald Sund. 31 through 41—Harald Sund. 46—Courtesy Mrs. Pierre Barnes and Mary Buell, published by permission of the University of Washington Press, Seattle, from *Across the Olympic Mountains* by Robert L. Wood, 1967. 49—Keith Gunnar. 50—Joseph Van Wormer from Bruce Coleman. 54, 55—Russ Lamb. 59—Sidney V. Bryant courtesy Mountaineers Archive, University of Washington Library. 60—Charles S. Gleason courtesy Mountaineers Archive, University of Washington Library. 61—Robert W. Kelley courtesy Washington State Historical Society, Tacoma. 62, 63—P. M. McGregor courtesy Mountaineers Archive, University of Washington Library; Asahel Curtis courtesy Mountaineers Archive, University of Washington Library; John A. Best Jr. courtesy Mountaineers Archive, University of Washington Library. 64, 65—Asahel Curtis courtesy Mountaineers Archive, University of Washington Library. 68—John V.A.F. Neal. 72, 73—Rare Book Division, The New York Public Library, Astor, Lenox and Tilden Foundations. 75—Picture Collection, The Branch Libraries, The New York Public Library. 78 through 89—David Cavagnaro. 92, 93—David Cavagnaro. 96—William W. Bacon III. 98, 99—Harald Sund. 105 through 115—Tom Tracy. 118—William W. Bacon III. 120, 121—William W. Bacon III. 126, 127—Tom Tracy. 131—Robert Waterman; Helen Cruickshank, The National Audubon Society—Kojo Tanaka from Animals Animals—R. Wayne Campbell. 135—Bob Miller, *Seattle Post Intelligencer*. 138—Jeff Foott from Bruce Coleman. 145 through 151—Robert Waterman. 154—D. C. Lowe. 156—D. C. Lowe. 161—Steven C. Wilson. 167 through 179—Steven C. Wilson.

Index

Numerals in italics indicate a photograph or drawing of the subject mentioned.

Filmsetting by C. E. Dawkins (Typesetters) Ltd., London, SE1 1UN.
Printed and bound in Belgium by Brepols S.A.—Turnhout.